"WE SHALL MEET AGAIN"

"WE SHALL MEET AGAIN"

THE FIRST BATTLE
OF MANASSAS (BULL RUN)

July 18–21, 1861

by
JoAnna M. McDonald

OXFORD
UNIVERSITY PRESS

OXFORD
UNIVERSITY PRESS

Athens Auckland Bangkok Bogotá Buenos Aires Calcutta
Cape Town Chennai Dar es Salaam Delhi Florence Hong Kong
Istanbul Karachi Kuala Lumpur Madrid Melbourne Mexico City
Mumbai Nairobi Paris São Paulo Shanghai Singapore Taipei Tokyo
Toronto Warsaw

and associated companies in
Berlin Ibadan

Originally published in cloth edition by White Mane Books
P.O. Box 152, 63 Burd Street, Shippensburg, Pennsylvania 17257

First published by Oxford University Press in paperback, 2000

Oxford is a registered trademark of Oxford University Press

Library of Congress Cataloging-in-Publication Data

McDonald, JoAnna M., 1970-
We shall meet again : the First Battle of Manassas (Bull Run), July 18–2 1, 1861 / by
JoAnna McDonald.
p. cm.
Includes bibliographical references (p.) and index.
ISBN 0-19-513938-0 (Pbk.)
1. Bull Run, 1st Battle of, Va., 1861. 1. Title.
E472.18 .M39 2000
973.7'31—dc21   99-088846

10 9 8 7 6 5 4 3 2 1

Printed in the United States of America

DEDICATION

To my parents, Norman and Barbara;
grandparents, Donald and Frances McDonald,
and to the nine hundred families who
lost loved ones at First Manassas.

FAR AWAY IN HUMBLE COTTAGE
SITS HIS MOTHER SAD AND LONE.
AND HER EYES ARE RED WITH WEEPING
THINKING OF HER ABSENT SON.

CONTENTS ─────────────

MAPS

PREFACE

On April 12, 1861, in Charleston harbor, South Carolina, Confederate Brigadier General Pierre Gustave Toutant Beauregard ordered the cannon to fire upon Fort Sumter. Within the garrison Major Robert Anderson commanded the Union soldiers. For thirty-three hours the Confederate batteries pounded the fort. Outnumbered, running low on ammunition and food, the exhausted Union men surrendered on April 14. There was no turning back. The American Civil War (also known as the War Between the States) had begun.*

For the most part the two sides were divided by regions, South and North. Eleven Southern states seceded from the Union; eighteen Northern states sided with the Federal Government. Three states, Missouri, Kentucky, and Maryland, were considered border (neutral) states. Citizens from these states joined either side, sometimes both. Settlers from Oregon and California returned to their native states and joined their respective regiments (see map 1).

---

*The Confederates concentrated forty-six cannon on Fort Sumter. The seventy-seven Union troops had only twenty-one cannon accessible.

MAP 1

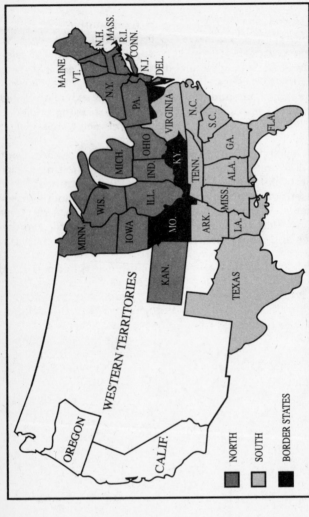

The Divided Union

In the spring of 1861 eleven Southern states seceded from the Union. Eighteen Northern states sided with the Federal Government. Three were considered border states: Missouri, Kentucky, and Maryland, and citizens from these states joined either side (sometimes both). Settlers from Oregon and California returned to their native states and joined their respective regiments.

ACKNOWLEDGEMENTS ————————————————————————

I would like to first thank my parents, family, and friends for supporting me through the long research and writing process. Two of the most influential historians in this project were Jim Burgess, Museum Director at the Manassas Battlefield Park, and John Hennessy, noted Civil War author. Jim provided excellent constructive criticism throughout my rewriting stage, and provided several photos from the Manassas archives. In addition, he took me on a guided tour of the area. John, as well, contributed some very helpful literary advice.

The Military History Institute's staff at the Carlisle Barracks, Carlisle, Pennsylvania again showed great cooperation.

In order to present the vast amount of photographs included within, a number of archives and individuals came to my assistance: the photo archives at the Military History Institute, Mike Winey and Randy Hackenburg curators; Mr. Ken Tilley of the Alabama Department of Archives and History sent me a photo of Colonel Egbert Jones, 4th Alabama. Mr. Robert Fouts of Alabama took the photo for me; Mr. John Bigham of the South Carolina Confederate Relic Room not only provided two photos, but he also sent me information pertaining to some of the South Carolina individuals who participated in the battle. Mr. Allen Stokes and Beth Bilderback of South Caroliniana Library, University of South Carolina, Columbia, South Carolina provided the photo of Colonel E.B.C. Cash, 8th South Carolina. Racine County Historical Society of Racine, Wisconsin and the Milwaukee Historical Society each provided one photo of soldiers from the 2d Wisconsin. Mr. William Gladstone of Florida also gave permission to use several of his impressive photos. Tom MacDonald and James Mundy, of Maine, each provided one photo of soldiers from the 2d Maine. The Library of Congress also supplied me two images; Mr. Ron Wilson from the Appomattox Court House National Park provided a slide of Mr. Wilmer McLean. And, while I did not get any photos from the Virginia Historical Society, Ms. AnnMarie F. Price was very helpful in finding photos from their collection. For a complete list of photographs and credits see page 209.

Lastly, I thank Jim Steinmetz and his wife of Steinmetz's photo shop, Carlisle, Pennsylvania. Jim developed all the photographs which I copied from the Military History Institute's collection.

INTRODUCTION

The First Battle of Manassas (also known as Bull Run) signified the beginning of the bloodiest war in America's history. From
June to July 1861, the South concentrated an army on the southern banks of Bull Run near Manassas Junction, Virginia.

Three months had passed since the Confederates had taken
Fort Sumter in South Carolina; Northern citizens demanded action. President Abraham Lincoln, therefore, ordered a Union force
to confront the Confederates amassing twenty-six miles southwest
of Washington, D.C. On Tuesday, July 16, the Union army moved
out of Alexandria, Virginia and Washington toward Manassas.

At 6:00 a.m., Sunday, July 21, Union artillery opened fire upon
Confederates deployed at the Stone Bridge about five miles southwest of Centreville, Virginia. After three hours, the battle progressed
to the Matthews Hill/Young's Branch area and continued for another three hours, until about noon, when the outnumbered Confederates retreated to Henry Hill. For an hour and a half (12:00–
1:30 p.m.) the Confederates organized a battle line along the southeastern edge of Henry Hill. From 1:30–4:30 p.m. the fight raged
around Henry Hill and the Chinn farm. By 4:30 p.m. the entire
Union army was in full retreat. The battlefield extended over a space
of three to five miles, and within this area nearly 30,000 soldiers
(15,000 Union and 14,000 Confederates) clashed.[1] While the fighting was often disorganized and clumsy, the soldiers endured their
baptism by fire. They were introduced to the horrors of war, and
learned to live with that knowledge.

Compared to subsequent Civil War battles the number of killed
(900) and wounded (3,000) at First Manassas seems minor. When
news of the day's fighting appeared in print, however, the civilian
population on both sides, rather than being alarmed, became angered and incited; they cried for more blood. No one in 1861 could
foresee the devastating casualty lists that would rise as the Northern and Southern armies met on the fields of battle.*

---

*To date, the strongest United States Army organized had been in the Mexican War (1846–1848).
It had numbered approximately 10,000 men. Moreover, the casualties in one of the largest
campaigns—which included four separate battles—added to a mere 2,700.[2]

"WE SHALL MEET AGAIN"

Chapter 1

WAYS AND MEANS

WEAPONS AT FIRST MANASSAS

Infantry

During this battle most of the infantrymen carried muzzle-loading smoothbore muskets with percussion ignition. A few regiments, however, shouldered the newer muzzle-loading rifles. To load both weapons the tactical manuals specified nine steps.

The .69 caliber smoothbore musket could be loaded with three types of ammunition: 1) a single round musket ball of .65 caliber, 2) "buck and ball"—three buckshot with a .65 caliber ball, 3) a cartridge containing twelve buckshot. The undersized ammunition facilitated loading. In this battle, however, a reduction in the rate of fire may have resulted from the soldiers' limited level of training and the antiquated condition of their weapons.

While undersized ammunition enabled a faster rate of fire, it made smoothbore muskets notoriously inaccurate. The tactics of massing a heavy concentration of firepower from line formations compensated for the poor accuracy of smoothbores. Buck and ball and buckshot cartridges also increased the chances of hitting opposing troops, but the smoothbore's effectiveness was still limited to ranges under 150 yards. In his memoirs Lieutenant General Ulysses S. Grant recalled a man with a smoothbore musket, a few hundred yards away, "might fire at you all day without you finding it out."[1]

In addition to poor accuracy, smoothbores tended to foul with black powder after only having been fired four or five times. When ignited, black powder leaves behind a heavy residue. The fouling builds up within the barrel with each shot, and after several rounds it becomes difficult to ram even an undersized ball down a dirty barrel. If the soldier was unable to ram the ball all the way down the barrel, the uncompressed powder burned even less efficiently, therefore the fouling increased. Ultimately, loading the musket became impossible. When faced with this dilemma, frustrated soldiers threw away their smoothbores and tried to find a more usable weapon on the battlefield.

The other infantry weapon used at First Manassas was the .58 caliber rifle-musket—adopted in 1855. Unlike older muzzle-loading rifles it was as fast and easy to load as a smoothbore musket with none of the smoothbore's disadvantages. The rifle-musket was effective out to 500 yards (or 900 yards if equipped with long range sights) against massed troops. In addition, it was much more accurate due to the rifling within the barrel.

Field Artillery

The cannon used at First Manassas were all muzzle-loading and, like the infantry weapons, either smoothbore or rifled. Smoothbore guns fired spherical projectiles with limited range and accuracy. Rifled artillery, however, could fire elongated projectiles with greater accuracy at ranges over a mile. The common denominator for both of these cannon was that they were direct fire weapons; to hit the target it had to be in view.[2]

UNIFORMS

At First Manassas neither side took the time to organize or furnish their troops with one common uniform; since the conflict was perceived to be of short duration, the color of one's outfit seemed of little significance. Moreover, in order to attract more recruits and media attention, commanders encouraged their units to have distinctive and multicolored uniforms. The gaudiest, the Zouave (zöö-av') costume, worn by both the Confederate and Union units, was modeled after the Algerian light infantrymen who served in the French Colonial Armies during the Crimean War (1853–56).

The "Tiger Rifles," Company B, belonged to Major Chatham Roberdeau Wheat's Special Battalion, Louisiana Volunteers. Many of these men had been recruited from the alleys and jails of New Orleans. A wealthy local businessman, A. Keene Richards, bought this unit their Zouave uniforms: scarlet skullcaps with long tassels, red shirts, blue or tan jackets, baggy trousers with blue and white stripes and white gaiters. In addition, on their hatbands they painted slogans: "Lincoln's Life or a Tiger's Death," "Tiger in Search of Abe," and, "Tiger in Search of a Black Republican."[3]

The "Maryland Guard," a company in the 1st Maryland Infantry Battalion, considered themselves a Zouave unit because on dress parade they wore a dark blue version of the uniform. Yet, on the field, they substituted their tight, short coats for a more generous blue jacket and black fitted trousers. Their outfit also included a blue kepi trimmed with yellow, and a blue undershirt.[4]

Among the Union Zouave units, two were heavily engaged: the 11th New York, and Company K, 69th New York, Captain Thomas Meagher's Zouaves. The 11th New York, nicknamed the "Fire Zouaves" because the majority of enlisted men had been firemen in New York City, shaved their heads like their Algerian counterparts. One even had his hair shaved in the form of an American Bald Eagle.[5] Because of the heat on July 21 the men did not wear their jackets. Most wore either red or light blue shirts, baggy, blue trousers and red fezs; the officers donned red kepis.[6] Meagher's Company K, 69th New York, uniform included short, dark blue jackets with red lace, baggy blue-gray pants and leather gaiters.[7] Like the 11th New York, many of the men removed their jackets and fought with their shirt sleeves rolled up to their elbows.

The "Red-Legged Devils," 14th Brooklyn Chasseurs dressed similarly to the Zouave style. Their uniform included red caps, red baggy trousers, short, blue jackets, and white gaiters. Chasseur and Zouave uniforms differed primarily in the cut of their coats and trousers and the color of their pants. (Traditionally, the French army utilized the Chasseurs as light infantry, equipped for reconnaissance and screening purposes. The Chasseur units during the Civil War, however, functioned as any other infantry regiment.)

In addition to the flamboyant Zouaves, several Union units went into battle wearing their gray state militia uniforms.

The Union regiments who were actively engaged at First Manassas and wore an entirely gray uniform were 2d Maine, 3d Maine, 5th Maine, 1st Massachusetts, 11th Massachusetts, 2d New Hampshire, 8th New York, 2d Wisconsin, and three companies in the 1st Minnesota.[8] Some regiments' dress, like the 1st and 2d Rhode Island, included gray pants and blue coats.[9]

To protect the back of the neck from the sun, havelocks (a flap of cloth which draped around the cap) were issued to the soldiers. The soldiers, however, found that the havelocks scratched the back of their necks. Consequently, many either threw them away or used them to bandage wounds.

Union regiments which did not don a gray uniform wore the volunteer regulation outfit: a blue forage cap (kepi), a dark-blue wool coat (the soldiers called this a blouse), with a flannel shirt underneath (red or gray or white), dark or sky-blue trousers, long-underwear, "drawers," wool socks, and short ankle boots.*

---

*(Throughout history many have assumed the 79th New York Highlanders wore their plaid pants or kilts during the battle. According to the regimental historian, and former Highlander, this unit dressed in the regulation volunteer outfit. They did not wear their dress parade kilts or plaid pants.)[10]

While most of the Confederate units wore gray or civilian clothes, some did have blue uniforms. Retired or displaced army officers dressed in their U.S. Regular Army dark blue uniforms— men like Brigadier General Thomas Jackson and Brigadier General Barnard Bee. Even Company A of the 2d Virginia donned a dark blue regular army uniform.[11] Young men, who had left their military schools, came dressed in "cadet gray" (blue-gray color). Others fought wearing a combination outfit: blue jacket, a white, blue or red undershirt, steel gray trousers and a kepi.

Once the battle began and smoke covered the area it was very difficult for the commanders to identify the enemy. Consequently, friendly fire killed or wounded many soldiers.

(Even after First Manassas one can find many cases where soldiers were wounded or killed by friendly fire in the preceding battles.)

U.S. Regulation Volunteer Uniform

**U.S. State Militia &
Confederate Uniform**
Union regiments in gray, 1st Massachusetts, 11th Massachusetts, 2d Maine, 3d Maine, 5th Maine, 2d New Hampshire, 8th New York, and 2d Wisconsin, and three companies in the 1st Minnesota.

11th New York
"Fire Zouaves"

14th Brooklyn Chasseurs
"Red-Legged Devils"

Tiger Rifles
Company B, Wheat's
Louisiana Battalion

FLAGS

Any large flag held by an infantryman was termed "color." (The cavalry units carried a "standard," a smaller flag.) Officially, the regiment had a national and regimental flag. Depending on the regiment and circumstances, they either took one flag or both into battle. The flag(s) would be positioned in the middle of the regiment and protected by the color guard (one sergeant and eight corporals). The purpose of the flag(s) was twofold. 1) It established a point of reference in the battle line. 2) It served as a rallying point for the soldiers.

In addition to their tactical usage the flag(s) represented the regiment and home. Local women provided many of the flags in

1861 and presented them to the men in special ceremonies. Disgrace fell upon the regiment if their flag was captured; seizing an opponent's colors, on the other hand, demonstrated a great and glorious accomplishment. Members of the guard rarely surrendered their flag without a hard fight; many, in fact, preferred to die in the melée rather than surrender their flag. A regiment was officially credited with advancing in battle to the farthest point that its flag reached—not necessarily the point at which the majority of its soldiers penetrated the enemies' line.[12]

Union-Confederate National Flags

Not only did the two opposing sides arrive at Manassas with similarly colored uniforms, but they also carried flags with corresponding colors. The "Stars and Stripes" represented the Union troops. In the Union (the blue corner of the flag) thirty-four stars represented the states; the formation of these stars varied in each flag. Thirteen horizontal stripes (red and white) stood for the original thirteen colonies. The colors red, white, and blue symbolized valor, purity, and truth, the true republican colors.

On the "Stars and Bars," the first Confederate national flag, the number of stars within the Union field depended on when the flag was made. Earlier versions had seven; as more Southern states seceded from the Union, additional stars appeared. The later ones had eleven. The stars formed a circle on a blue field and represented the motto "You defend me and I'll protect you." There were three horizontal stripes of equal width—red, white, and red. The three bars stood for the state, church, and press. Red signified the state and free speech; white represented the church, and blue—truth—bound the colors together.[13]

The "Stars and Bars" was not the only Confederate flag on the field. In many regiments each company carried its own unique flag.

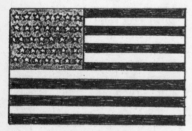

Stars and Stripes   **Stars and Bars**

Distance and battle smoke limited one's ability to differentiate the flags. To compound the problem, the hot July day produced little breeze, and the flags hung limp. Identifying a unit was almost impossible, unless one studied the area with field glasses (binoculars). In many circumstances, however, the officers did not have time to scrutinize the situation. Consequently officers shouted conflicting orders due to the ambiguity of identification; participants became frustrated and confused.

After the battle, General Beauregard consulted with several Confederate officers concerning a new battle flag, which, by the following campaign, had been adopted.[14]

The flag of the Army of Northern Virginia, with the Saint-Andrews Cross
Eleven stars represent the Confederates states, the two extra stars are for Kentucky and Missouri. The Confederates claimed these two states as well; however, they were officially considered neutral.

COMMANDERS

Confederate

Brigadier General P.G.T. Beauregard,
age 43*
(Seen in his major general's uniform)

General Joseph E. Johnston,
age 54

Brigadier General P.G.T. Beauregard graduated second out of a class of forty-five at West Point in 1838. He stood five-feet, seven-inches, weighed about 150 pounds, had an olive complexion and graying hair. At the age of forty-three, he was the first Confederate given the rank of brigadier general.[15]

During the Mexican War he served as an engineer on Lieutenant General Winfield Scott's staff. In early February 1861, the Louisian-ian resigned from the United States Army. On February 26, Confed-erate President Jefferson Davis invited him to take command of the South Carolina forces confronting Fort Sumter. After the surrender of the fort they nicknamed him "Hero of Sumter." Though having commanded only approximately 80–100 men during his military ca-reer, Davis assigned Beauregard the significant command of the army (eventually numbering 24,240) near Manassas Junction, Virginia.[16]

West Pointer, and Virginian, General Joseph Eggleston Johnston, class of 1829, graduated thirteenth out of forty-six. He was of medium height, trim, and had gray eyes. His previous war

---

* The ages herein indicate their age in 1861. This is not necessarily their age in the photograph.

experiences included the Black Hawk War, the Seminole War, the Mexican War, and the Utah Expedition. He had been wounded five times in the Mexican War and awarded three brevets—honorary promotions in rank. After thirty years service with the United States Army he resigned his commission on April 22, 1861, and joined the Confederacy. At the age of fifty-four the Confederacy gave him the rank of brigadier general and assigned him command of the soldiers at Harpers Ferry. In early June, Union troops invaded the northeastern region of the Shenandoah Valley. To meet this new threat, Johnston directed his force to confront them.[17]

Union

Brigadier General Irvin McDowell,
age 43
(Engraving)

Compared to his opposition and fellow alumni of West Point, forty-three-year-old, blue-eyed, Irvin McDowell was a big man at six-feet and, as a result of his voracious appetite, also a heavy man.

Although McDowell never commanded more than eight men, President Lincoln was impressed by his military education. McDowell studied at a military school in France (College de Troyes) and spent a year observing French military tactics. After his stay in France, he attended West Point and graduated the same year as Beauregard, 1838, ranked twenty-third in his class of forty-five. From 1841 to 1845, he taught military tactics to the cadets at West

Point. During the Mexican War he worked as aide-de-camp (secretary) for General J.E. Wool and for General Winfield Scott's staff. On May 14, 1861, McDowell received the rank of brigadier general and command of the Union forces assembling in Washington, D.C.[18]

ORGANIZATION OF THE ARMIES

Two Confederate forces united at Manassas: the Army of the Potomac and the Army of the Shenandoah. Beauregard commanded the Army of the Potomac, which consisted of seven brigades and several unattached units. Johnston led the Shenandoah army comprised of four brigades. Each brigade, then, consisted of three to five regiments.

Five divisions* constituted McDowell's Union force, the Army of Northeastern Virginia. Two to four brigades made up a division and each brigade had three to six regiments/battalions. A battalion was a compilation of companies numbering less than a regiment. For example, Major George Sykes commanded a battalion of U.S. Regular infantry. It consisted of two companies from the Second U.S. Infantry regiment, five companies from the Third U.S. Infantry regiment, and one company from the Eighth U.S. Infantry regiment.

---

*Following the First Battle of Manassas, the names of these armies changed. The Confederate force in Virginia became known as the Army of Northern Virginia and the Northern force (fighting the Army of Northern Virginia in the east) the Army of the Potomac.

Army of the Potomac (C.S.A.)
Brigadier General Pierre G.T. Beauregard*

First Brigade (5)†: 4,961   Second Brigade (3): 2,444

**Brigadier General
Milledge Luke Bonham, age 48**
Resident of South Carolina and attended
South Carolina College; fought in the Seminole and Mexican War; appointed brigadier
general April 23, 1861. Resigned January
1862 and served as governor of South Carolina 1862–64.[19]

(In civilian attire)

**Brigadier General
Richard Stoddert Ewell, age 44**
Resident of Washington, D.C.; graduated
from West Point 1840, 13/40. Served in
Mexican War and frontier; resigned May 7,
1861; appointed a Virginian and given the
rank of brigadier general June 17, 1861.
(Seen in his major general's uniform)

Third Brigade (3): 2,121

Brigadier General James Longstreet, age 40
Born in South Carolina; family moved to Alabama.
Graduated West Point 1842, 54/62, classmates with
Beauregard and McDowell. Fought in the Mexican War
and on the frontier. Appointed brigadier general June
17, 1861.

---

*Brigadier General David Rumph Jones also commanded the Fourth Brigade (5): 3,528, at
Manassas. His photograph is unavailable at this time. Resident of South Carolina; graduated
West Point 1846, 41/59; served in the Mexican War and frontier; commissioned brigadier general
June 17, 1861. Died of heart trouble January 15, 1863.

†The number in parentheses represents the number of regiments in each brigade. For the complete
listing of regiments and regimental commanders see the Order of Battles, appendix III, p. 186.

Fifth Brigade (5): 3,276

**Colonel Philip St. George Cocke,
age 52**
Graduated from West Point 1832, 6/45; resigned in 1834. Became president of the Virginia Agricultural Society. After First Manassas he was promoted to brigadier general, October 1861. Yet, after only eight months service he retired due to poor health. On December 26, 1861, he killed himself.

Sixth Brigade (3): 2,620

Colonel Jubal Anderson Early, age 45
West Point graduate, 1837, 18/50. Served in the Seminole War and resigned in 1838. He became a lawyer but at the outbreak of the Mexican War he again fought for his country. Although he voted against Virginia's secession, he joined the Confederate army, and served as a competent leader.

Seventh Brigade (2): 1,100

Colonel Nathan George Evans, age 37
Attended Randolph-Macon College but transferred to West Point, graduated in 1848, 36/38. His fellow cadets nicknamed him "Shanks" because he had very skinny legs. Served on the frontier and in the Indian Wars, he resigned in February 1861. Fellow Confederate officers thought he was arrogant and crude and he liked to drink. In fact he made a Prussian orderly follow him with a jug of whiskey. Nevertheless, he was extremely brave, brash, and independent.
(Seen in his brigadier general's uniform)

Reserve Brigade (2): 1,355

**Brigadier General
Theophilus Hunter Holmes, age 57**
Born in North Carolina; graduated from West Point in 1829, 44/46. Served in the Mexican War and on the frontier. He resigned from the U.S. Army on April 22, 1861. Jefferson Davis appointed him brigadier general on June 5, 1861.

*Unbrigaded Unit**

Hampton's Legion: 654

Colonel Wade Hampton, age 43
Graduated from South Carolina College in
1836. One of South Carolina's finest aristo-
crats and intellectuals. He was a wealthy
plantation owner and a South Carolina poli-
tician. At the outbreak of the war he organized and financed a legion and served as
its colonel during First Manassas.

Artillery:

35 guns:

    22 six-pounder smoothbore guns,
      3 six-pounder rifled guns,
      6 ten-pounder Parrott rifles,
      4 twelve-pounder field howitzers.

Total: 24,240[20]

---

*Major Julien Harrison's Virginia cavalry battalion (four companies) was also ordered to report to Brigadier General Bonham on May 27, 1861.

Army of the Shenandoah (C.S.A.)

General Joseph E. Johnston

First Brigade (5): 2,611

Second Brigade (5): 2,546

**Brigadier General
Thomas Jonathan Jackson, age 37**
Graduated West Point 1846, 17/59. Received two brevets for distinguished service in the Mexican War. Resigned in 1851 and taught at the Virginia Military Institute. He was appointed brigadier general on June 17, 1861, and became one of America's greatest leaders.
(Seen in his lieutenant general's uniform)

**Colonel Francis Stebbins Bartow,
age 44**
He was a lawyer, legislator, and Confederate congressman. He recruited and served as the captain of "Oglethorpe Rifles," Company B, 8th Georgia, and soon became the colonel of the 8th Georgia. Although his brigade consisted of five regiments only two (7th and 8th Georgia) participated in the battle.

Third Brigade (4): 2,790

Fourth Brigade (4): 2,250

**Brigadier General
Barnard Elliot Bee, age 37**
Native of Charleston, South Carolina; West Point graduate, 1845, 33/41; served on the frontier and in the Mexican War. Awarded two brevets and was wounded once. He resigned in March 1861, and appointed brigadier general in the Confederate army June 17, 1861.

Colonel Arnold Elzey, age 45
Born in Somerset County, Maryland; graduated from West Point in 1837, 33/50. Received a brevet in the Mexican War. Resigned his commission April 1861; appointed colonel of the 1st Maryland, and shortly after given command of the fourth brigade.
(Seen in his brigadier general's uniform)

Unbrigaded Unit

1st Virginia Cavalry (Ten companies)

Colonel James Ewell Brown Stuart, age 28
"Jeb" was born in Patrick County, Virginia. He graduated from West Point in 1854, 13/46. He served on
the frontier where he was seriously wounded. Resigned
his captain's commission in May 1861 and became
one of the Confederacy's most talented cavaliers. In
a later campaign, he fought against his father-in-law,
Philip St. George Cooke, who served with the Union
"Army of the Potomac."

(Seen in his general's uniform)

Artillery:
   20 guns, 19 six-pounder smoothbore guns and 1 twelve-
pounder field howitzer

Total: 10,961

Grand Total: 29,949

******

   While the combined Confederate forces totalled almost 30,000,
the actual troops directly involved in the fighting numbered approximately 14,050. The remaining units either arrived too late at
the scene or were guarding the right flank.[21]

The Army of Northeastern Virginia (U.S.A.)

Brigadier General Irvin McDowell

First Division (4)*: 9,936   Second Division (2): 2,485

**Brigadier General
Daniel Tyler, age 62**

Born in Brooklyn, Connecticut in 1799. Attended West Point and graduated in 1819, 14/29. Served in garrison and was also sent to France to study their artillery tactics. In 1834 he resigned. He unsuccessfully worked in the manufacture of pig iron but was more successful in the railroad business. For five years he served as the president of the Macon & Western Railroad in Georgia. At the outbreak of war, he returned to Connecticut, and received a brigadier general commission, commanding Connecticut volunteers, May 1861.

Colonel David Hunter, age 59

Graduated West Point 1822, 25/40. Served on the frontier, resigned in 1836, but returned during the Mexican War—acting as paymaster. In 1860 he began correspondence with newly elected President Lincoln, and received an invitation to accompany the president on the inaugural train to Washington. He was promoted to colonel May 1861.

(Seen in his major general's uniform)

Third Division (3): 9,062   Fifth Division (2)†: 6,173

Colonel Samuel Peter Heintzelman, age 56

Born in Manheim, Pennsylvania. Appointed to West Point at the age of seventeen, and graduated in 1826, 17/41. Served on the frontier and was awarded a brevet to major in the Mexican War.

Colonel Dixon S. Miles, age 57

Born in Maryland. Graduated from West Point on July 1, 1824. Served with the 7th Infantry on the frontier and in the Mexican War. Brevet major, May 9, 1846, for gallant and distinguished conduct in the defense of Fort Brown, Texas. Became colonel of 2d Infantry, January 19, 1859.

---

*The numbers in the parentheses indicate the brigades in each division. For the Union Order of Battles see appendix III, p. 191.

†Colonel Miles' division acted as reserves near Centreville, Virginia. Brigadier General Theodore Runyon's Fourth Division acted as reserves near Alexandria, Virginia.

Artillery:
57 cannon:

    1 rifled thirty-pounder;
    2 rifled twenty-pounders;
  10 rifled thirteen-pounders;
  16 rifled ten-pounders;
    8 twelve-pounders (smoothbore) Field Howitzers;
    4 twelve-pounders (smoothbore) Napoleons
  14 smoothbore six-pounders;
    2 small boat twelve-pounders (smoothbore) Howitzers

Total: 35,732

******

On July 21, however, only about 13,000–15,000 men actually participated in the fighting. The remaining troops McDowell either did not effectively use or many men dropped out, too exhausted from marching, or were held in reserve.

STRATEGIES AND INITIAL BATTLE PLANS

Confederate

On June 2, Beauregard assumed command of the troops stationed near Manassas Junction. This position was strategically significant for several reasons:

1) Two railroads, the Manassas Gap and the Orange and Alexandria, connected at this junction. Most importantly, the Manassas Gap railroad linked Johnston's forces (seventy miles away in the Shenandoah Valley) with Beauregard's. If Union commander McDowell threatened Beauregard's position, Johnston could reinforce Beauregard by rail via the Manassas Gap railroad. In addition, the trains could bring food supplies from the rich surrounding farm lands and troops from Richmond.[22]

2) Since Manassas is only twenty-six miles from Washington, D.C., Beauregard could easily observe the Union army's movements and its growing strength.

On July 16, a month after he took command, Beauregard proposed a grand and complex strategic plan to Davis:

A: Johnston should unite the bulk of his force with Beauregard at Manassas. The combined armies would engage (defeat and capture) McDowell's force near Fairfax Court-House, Virginia.

B: Johnston, with part of Beauregard's force, would return to the Shenandoah Valley and crush the Union force stationed there.

C: After destroying these Union armies, Johnston would reinforce Confederate troops in West Virginia and rout the Union soldiers based in this vicinity.

D: Johnston's combined force would then attack Washington,
D.C., from the rear while Beauregard made a frontal assault. Under the weight of a two-pronged attack the capital would surrender
and the war would be over (see map 2).

Davis tactfully declined this plan for several reasons: lack of
transportation, the danger of Union troops cutting off communications with their men in the Shenandoah Valley (after Johnston moved
out), and the fact that they did not yet have enough soldiers to
implement the proposal. For the present Davis ordered Beauregard
to stay on the defensive and wait for McDowell's army to make the
first move.[23]

MAP 2

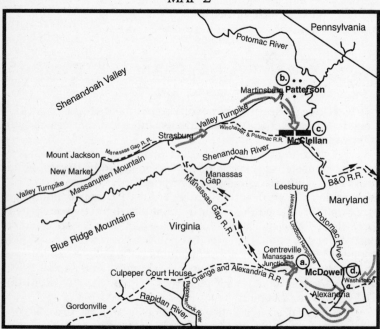

Beauregard's master plan, July 16, 1861

**a: Johnston's and Beauregard's combined forces destroy McDowell's Union
army. b: Johnston, with part of Beauregard's force, returns to the Shenandoah
Valley and crushes Patterson's Union army. c: Johnston moves down the Valley to West Virginia, breaks McClellan's Union force. d: Johnston and Beauregard
surround and capture Washington, D.C.**

Union

Major General
Robert Patterson, age 69
Patterson served with Scott during the
Mexican War.

(Postwar)

Lieutenant General
Winfield Scott, age 75
In 1861 he was the commander in chief of
all the Union forces.

After two months of inaction following the Sumter incident, the Northern states grew restless and demanded that the Union army move on Richmond, the Confederate capital. Yet, McDowell, unwilling to engage the enemy with raw recruits, regarded the men as little more than civilians dressed in uniforms. They required more training, drilling, and conditioning. The public did not understand or sympathize. Subsequently, Lincoln pressured McDowell to engage the enemy.

Knowing Beauregard's army was deployed on the southern banks of Bull Run, McDowell initially planned to turn the Confederate right flank, crush Beauregard's force and capture Richmond. Meanwhile, in the Shenandoah Valley, Union Major General Robert Patterson's army (18,000) was sent to detain and destroy Johnston's force (10,000), a significant assignment because without Johnston's reinforcements Beauregard would be outnumbered by approximately three-to-one. Patterson's intelligence, however, magnified the Confederate forces four times; he repeatedly hesitated to attack. In fact, on July 17, Patterson retreated seven miles. On Thursday, July 18, he reported to his commanding officer, Lieutenant General Winfield Scott, "The enemy has stolen no march upon me. I have kept him actively employed, and by threats and reconnaissances in force caused him to be re-enforced."[24] Patterson was sorely mistaken. The leading elements of Johnston's army arrived at Piedmont Station early Friday morning and began boarding the train for Manassas Junction. That same day the first Confederate reinforcements disembarked at Manassas (see map 3).

MAP 3

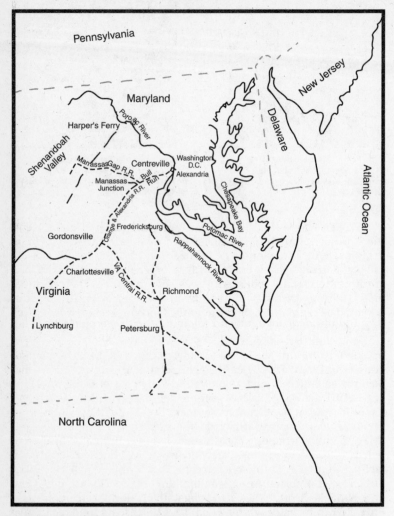

Pennsylvania

Maryland

New Jersey

Delaware

Potomac River

Harper's Ferry

Shenandoah Valley

Manassas Gap R.R.

Centreville

Washington D.C.

Alexandria

Manassas Junction

Bull Run

Orange & Alexandria R.R.

Chesapeake Bay

Atlantic Ocean

Fredericksburg

Gordonsville

Rappahannock River

Charlottesville

Va Central R.R.

Virginia

Richmond

Lynchburg

Petersburg

North Carolina

Johnston reinforces Beauregard's army via Manassas Gap R.R.
For the first time in military history the railroads played a significant role in war time strategy and logistics.

VIGNETTE:
A SOLDIER'S LAST LETTER HOME.

To help pass the time in camp many soldiers wrote their loved ones. On Sunday, July 14, thirty-two-year-old Major Sullivan Ballou, 2d Rhode Island, sat down and penned a letter to his wife.

My very dear Sarah:

The indications are very strong that we shall move in a few days— perhaps tomorrow. Lest I should not be able to write again, I feel impelled to write a few lines that may fall under your eye when I shall be no more. Our movements may be of a few days duration and full of pleasure—and it may be one of some conflict and death to me. 'Not my will, but thine, O God be done.' If it is necessary that I should fall on the battle field for my Country, I am ready.

I have no misgivings about, or lack of confidence in the cause in which I am engaged, and my courage does not halt or falter. I know how strongly American Civilization now leans on the triumph of the Government, and how great a debt we owe to those who went before us through the blood and sufferings of the Revolution. And I am willing—perfectly willing—to lay down all my joys in this life, to help maintain this Government, and to pay that debt.

But my dear wife, when I know that with my own joys, I lay down nearly all of your's, and replace them in this life with cares and sorrows, when after having eaten for long years the bitter fruits of orphanage myself, I must offer it as the only sustenance to my dear little children, is it weak or dishonorable, that while the banner of my forefathers floats calmly and fondly in the breeze, underneath my unbounded love for you, my darling wife and children should struggle in fierce, though useless contests with love of Country...

...Sarah my love for you is deathless, it seems to bind me with mighty cables that nothing but Omnipotence could break; and yet my love of Country comes over me like a strong wind and burns me unresistably on with all these chains to the battle field...

Major Sullivan Ballou

...But, O Sarah! if the dead can come back to this earth and flit unseen around those they loved, I shall always be near you; in the gladest days and in the darkest nights, advised to your happiest scenes and gloomiest hours, always, always, and if there be a soft breeze upon your cheek, it shall be my breath, as the cool air fans your throbbing temple, it shall be my spirit passing by. Sarah do not mourn me dead; think I am gone and wait for thee, for we shall meet again...

Sullivan[25]

Seven days later, during the First Battle of Manassas, the 2d Rhode Island fought against Wheat's Louisiana battalion, 4th South Carolina, 4th Alabama, 2d and 11th Mississippi and especially the 8th Georgia. While repositioning the regiment, an artillery shell tore Major Sullivan Ballou's leg off. He was mortally wounded, and his men carried him to the Sudley Church where he died. Union troops buried Sullivan and the body of his colonel, John Slocum, in shallow graves.

In the weeks and months which followed, some victorious Confederates, consumed with anger and seeking revenge for their fallen comrades, desecrated the graves of many Union soldiers. A year later, 1862, the Confederates evacuated Manassas, and the Union army returned to the battlefield. Members from the 2d Rhode Island, accompanied by Governor William Sprague of Rhode Island, looked for the graves of their men. One Negro girl led them to the charred remains of a headless body. Upon inspection of the uniform they determined that the mutilated body was Sullivan Ballou. The young girl told the Rhode Islanders that some Georgia boys cut his head off and burned the body. Horrified, Sprague searched for more eyewitnesses to corroborate her story. In their investigation they found three eyewitnesses, a fourteen-year-old boy, a farmer named Newman, and a woman who nursed the sick and wounded at Sudley Church. The woman begged the Confederate soldiers not to desecrate the body, but the men mocked her. She was able, however, to save a lock of Ballou's hair. Sprague and his men determined that the Georgia boys, terribly shot up by the 2d Rhode Island at First Manassas, sought revenge on Colonel Slocum, and mistakenly mutilated Major Ballou's body. Later, the Rhode Islanders exhumed and identified Colonel Slocum's body in a shallow grave.[26]

THE MARCH TO MANASSAS
"the heat and suffocating dust soon began to tell"

At two-o'clock, Tuesday afternoon, July 16, the Union army moved out of Washington and Alexandria, Virginia. At first, the men sang "Old Virginny" and "Dixie." The cheers and singing, however, soon ceased. Private Martin A. Haynes of the 2d New Hampshire recalled:

> ...the heat and suffocating dust soon began to tell upon the men, not yet hardened for such a march, and many were obliged to fall out of the ranks and seek shade and rest.
>
> The bivouac that night was at Bailey's Cross Roads, and the march resumed early the next morning. Evidences of the recent presence of the enemy were met, the road having been obstructed at places by felled trees, and the pioneers of the Second—a select squad of twenty men under charge of a sergeant—found plenty of exercise in clearing the way for the column.[27]

Tired and undisciplined, the soldiers stopped frequently to rest and plunder Virginia farms. Colonel William T. Sherman's aides galloped along the roadside and shouted to his brigade, "Colonel Sherman says you must keep in the ranks; you must close up; you must not chase the pigs and chickens." The men disregarded their orders and defiantly shouted, "Tell Colonel Sherman we will get all the water, pigs and chickens we want." While resting at Germantown, the 79th New York "Highlanders," one of four regiments in Sherman's brigade, discovered several beehives which they quickly overturned. Private William Todd later described the scene:

> ...then began the scramble for the honey. But: 'As Bees bizz out wi' angry fyke, When plundering herds assail their byke,' the air was soon 'blue' with bees, curses and imprecations; men ran hither and thither trying to shake off their tormentors, while mounted officers put spurs to their horses and beat a hasty retreat.[28]

Having been defeated by the angry bees, one 79th officer ran after a plump pig.

> One of our own officers, even, did not escape ridicule, which, however, he invited. Captain —— had insisted on wearing the kilts when we started on the march. "The

Highlanders," he said, "wear the kilts in India, and surely the gnats and mosquitoes of Virginia are not so troublesome as the venomous insects of the East." Being the only member thus arrayed he was a conspicuous figure. His love for fresh pork, and utter disregard of orders, led him, with drawn sword, to give chase to a young pig. The chase was an exciting one; as the captain ran, his kilts flew up, and his long, gaunt legs were exposed. "Put on your drawers!" "Take off that petticoat!" "Put on your pants!" And, as the race continued: "Go it, piggy!" and "Catch him Captain," resounded from the ranks of interested spectators. The climax was reached when the porker, hard pressed, ran through a snake fence. As the pig squeezed under the lowest rail the captain threw himself over the top one, and in the act made such a exhibition of his attenuated anatomy as to call forth a roar of laughter from all who witnessed it, and the cries of "Take off that petticoat!" and "Put on your pants!" were repeated. The captain appeared the next morning in ordinary uniform.[29] [And, the pig got away.]

For their absurd and undisciplined behavior Sherman nicknamed the 79th the "New York rowdies."[30]

After two days of slow, tedious marching, the vanguard of the Union army—Sherman's and Colonel Israel Richardson's brigades—arrived in Centreville, Virginia.

Private Martin Haynes, age 19
2d New Hampshire

THE BATTLE AT BLACKBURN'S FORD

JULY 18, THURSDAY (12:00 P.M.–4:00 P.M.)
"Do not bring on an engagement..."

OPPOSING COMMANDERS

CONFEDERATE

Brigade Commander:

Brigadier General James Longstreet
3,528

Brigade Commander:

Colonel Jubal Early
1,500

UNION

Division Commander:

Brigadier General Daniel Tyler
9,936

Brigade Commander:

Colonel Israel Richardson
3,920*

*Only approximately 1,500 Union troops actually fought in this battle.

25

At 8:15 a.m., Thursday, July 18, McDowell wrote the following directive to his lead division commander, Brigadier General Daniel Tyler:

> GENERAL: I have information which leads me to believe you will find no force at Centreville, and will meet with no resistance in getting there.
> Observe well the roads to Bull Run and to Warrenton. Do not bring on an engagement, but keep up the impression that we are moving on Manassas.[1]

An hour later, Tyler's lead brigade entered Centreville and found the Confederates had retreated toward Mitchell's and Blackburn's Ford. "Desiring to ascertain the extent" of the Confederate force near these fords, Tyler directed his lead brigade, commanded by Colonel Israel Richardson, down the Manassas-Centreville road.[2] It was now 10:00 a.m. After two hours Tyler ordered six cannon to unlimber on the northern ridge, about one-and-a-half miles away from the fords. At 12:00 p.m. the Union cannoneers opened fire on Mitchell's and Blackburn's Fords. Tyler hoped the Confederates would return fire so he could assess their infantry strength and battery positions. Yet, for nearly half-an-hour the Confederate guns were silent. Finally, at 12:30 p.m., Confederate artilleryman Captain Del Kemper fired back six shots and then retreated across Mitchell's Ford.

On the southern bank of Blackburn's Ford Confederate Brigadier General James Longstreet's outnumbered infantrymen hid silently in the bushes. If they returned fire the Union commander would be able to calculate Longstreet's weakness; and the enemy could either report their findings, or press their attack and break through the Confederate position.

Frustrated that the cannon barrage had not provoked a Confederate response, Tyler ordered a make-shift infantry battalion and three companies from the 1st Massachusetts toward Blackburn's Ford (see map 4). The 1st Massachusetts men, dressed in gray uniforms, entered the wooded area fronting the ford. There they discovered the disconcerting fact that the Confederate skirmishers also wore gray. Aware that other Union units were dressed in gray, Lieutenant William H.B. Smith ran forward and exclaimed, "Who are you?"

The Confederates replied, "Who are you?"

Incautiously and naively, Smith answered, "Massachusetts men..."

MAP 4

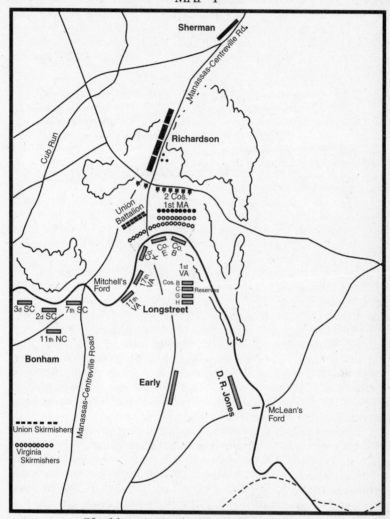

Blackburn's Ford • Thursday, July 18

Tyler deploys one Union brigade near Blackburn's Ford. After nearly half-an-hour of cannonading Confederate Captain Del Kemper returns fire. Outnumbered, he withdraws his guns across Mitchell's Ford. Near Blackburn's Ford, Union and Confederate skirmishers battle. The Virginians, however, are overwhelmed, and they retreat across Bull Run.

Immediately, a volley came from the Confederate line, and Lieutenant Smith was killed instantly.[3] The Massachusetts men met skirmishers from the 1st Virginia. After several rounds the outnumbered Virginians retreated across Blackburn's Ford. To the left of the 1st Virginia, men from the 11th Virginia nervously listened and watched. Orderly Sergeant William H. Morgan, 11th Virginia, recalled:

> *...All nerves were strung to a high tension. We were on the eve of a battle, a sure enough battle in which men would be wounded and killed, and who would be the victims no one knew...I saw many pale faces; don't know how I looked, but felt rather pale.*[4]

Along Longstreet's line the concealed Virginians fired scattering shots at the Union skirmishers.

Tyler, still dissatisfied with the Confederate response, ordered two cannon to join the infantry near the ford.[5] The artillerymen rode down from the ridge and unlimbered about 500 yards from Bull Run. To support the two guns, Union Colonel Richardson sent in the 12th New York.

With his center threatened, Longstreet directed the four remaining companies from the 1st Virginia into the fray (see map 5). The Virginians poured volley after volley into the Union artillerymen. The artillerymen, in the open field, withdrew. To avoid the missiles, the 12th New York fell to the ground and attempted to fire from a prone position. None of the New Yorkers, however, had practiced the difficult task of loading a musket while lying down. One soldier accidentally shot himself in the face.[6] For nearly twenty minutes the 12th and the other Union skirmishers fought. In the confusion a New York captain ordered his company to retreat. The remaining New York companies soon followed.[7]

Seeing the Union troops falling back, Longstreet directed his Virginia regiments to pursue them. As the Virginians crossed the creek, Confederate Colonel Jubal Early's brigade and seven cannon arrived. Early shouted, "Now boys, if you don't run, the Yankees will." A Confederate captain directed a company to load in nine times, as Hardee's manual taught. Early yelled, "Load nine times? Hell and damnation! Load in the most expeditious manner possible."[8] Accordingly, the men loaded and fired as fast as they could.

On the northern bank of Bull Run the Union skirmishers, flanked by the Virginians, fell back to the main Union line. With the 12th New York gone, the Confederates struck at the 1st Massachusetts' left flank. The 1st, however, along with two Michigan

MAP 5

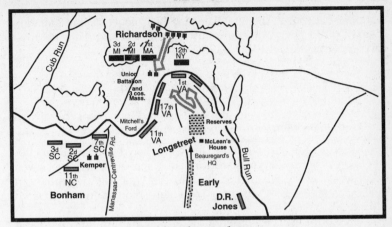

The battle escalates.

Seeking to provoke a reaction from the Confederates, Union commanders send two cannon closer to the bank of Bull Run. In addition, the 12th New York joins the attack. With the Confederate center threatened, Longstreet sends in his reserves.

MAP 6

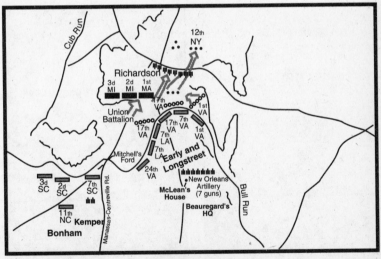

Counterattack

Due to battle confusion the 12th New York retreats without orders. At the same time the 1st and 17th Virginia counterattack. Confederate Colonel Jubal Early arrives with reinforcements along with seven cannon from a New Orleans battery.

regiments, stayed in the fight (see map 6). Colonel Richardson suggested to Tyler that they counterattack with these three regiments. Later Tyler explained:

> ...the enemy [was] in large force and strongly fortified, and a further attack was unnecessary; ...it was merely a reconnaissance which [I] had made; [I] found where the strength of the enemy lay, and ordered [our men] to fall back in good order to our batteries on the hill...[9]

The Union regiments, therefore, fell back. For the next hour, 3:00-4:00 p.m., the artillerymen continued a spirited duel. The seven Confederate guns, which belonged to the Washington Artillery of New Orleans, fired 310 rounds. The eight Union cannon answered with 415.[10]

By 4:00 p.m. Tyler ordered the artillerymen to limber up and return to Centreville. Colonel Sherman's brigade covered the retreat. After four hours of fighting the first encounter at Manassas was over. The Confederates reported sixty-three killed and wounded. Tyler calculated nineteen killed, thirty-eight wounded and twenty-six missing (see map 7).[11]

Lieutenant William H.B. Smith
1st Massachusetts

Orderly Sergeant William H. Morgan
11th Virginia

(Postwar)

MAP 7

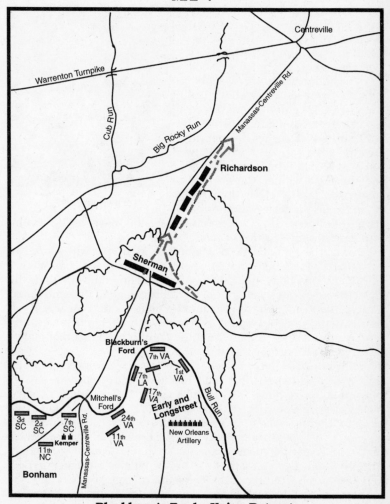

Centreville

Warrenton Turnpike

Cub Run

Big Rocky Run

Manassas-Centreville Rd.

Richardson

Sherman

Blackburn's
Ford

7th VA

7th
LA

1st
VA

17th
VA

Mitchell's
Ford

Early and
Longstreet

Bull Run

3d
SC

2d
SC

7th
SC

Kemper

24th
VA

11th
NC

11th
VA

New Orleans
Artillery

Manassas-Centreville Rd.

Bonham

Blackburn's Ford • Union Retreat

**After four hours of skirmishing the Union troops retreat back to Centreville,
Virginia.**

VIGNETTE:
MR. WILMER MCLEAN

During the battle at Blackburn's Ford Beauregard used Mr.
Wilmer McLean's house as his
headquarters. As the artillery
barrage raged, one shell crashed
into the chimney and threw rubble
into the iron kettle of stew. The
stew and fragments scattered
everywhere; McLean's kitchen
was ruined along with General
Beauregard's supper. Fortunately
for the McLean family no one was
hurt because Wilmer McLean had
taken his family from the area
prior to the battle. In addition to

Wilmer McLean

using his house, the Confederates used his barn as a hospital
and a prison for captured Union soldiers.

After the First Battle of Manassas, McLean's wife moved to
Appomattox (125 miles away) where friends resided, but Wilmer
returned to his home near Manassas Junction and worked for the
Confederate quartermaster until February 28, 1862. A month later,
March, the Confederates evacuated Manassas and McLean's job
opportunities ended. Wishing to reunite with his family and find a
more peaceful area, remote from the fighting, McLean made himself comfortable at Appomattox, Virginia.

Three years later, 1865, the opposing armies once again met
near McLean's house—this time 125 miles south of Manassas at
his Appomattox home. On Palm Sunday Union officers asked
McLean where Confederate General Robert E. Lee and Union Lieutenant General Ulysses S. Grant could meet. McLean showed the
officers a run down, wretched house; the officers declined. Reluctantly, McLean offered his home as a meeting place. On Sunday,
April 9, 1865, Lee and Grant sat in Mr. Wilmer McLean's parlor,
and Lee surrendered the Army of Northern Virginia to Grant.

Ironically, the war began near Wilmer McLean's house at
Manassas Junction and ended in his parlor four years later, and
although the later meeting was more serene, McLean fell victim to
Union souvenir hunters. Union officers stripped his house; they
stole the marble-topped table on which the surrender papers had
been signed (the surrender-table) and even a small rag doll which

had lain on the parlor floor. Soldiers waiting outside picked McLean's flowers to send back home. To recover his losses McLean tried to establish a lithograph business which depicted the surrender scene. Unfortunately, the business failed, and McLean eventually sold his Appomattox house* and returned to his birth place in Alexandria, Virginia.[12]

---

*(Part of the McLean house still stands at Manassas today. For directions to his house please ask at the Manassas National Battlefield. One can also visit his house at Appomattox Courthouse; for directions contact the National Park Service, U.S. Department of the Interior or the Virginia Commerce Department.)

Chapter 3

REVISED BATTLE PLANS

Major John Barnard
McDowell's Chief of Engineers

Governor William Sprague
of Rhode Island

While the casualties at Blackburn's Ford were relatively light, Tyler's "reconnaissance" showed that the Confederate center and right flank were too strong to turn. In addition, the country roads in this area were too narrow and crooked for maneuvering large columns of troops. With this unforeseen complication McDowell reevaluated his battle strategy.

On July 19, Major John G. Barnard, chief engineer, accompanied by Governor William Sprague of Rhode Island, and a company of cavalry, reconnoitered the Confederate left flank. Two or three miles above the Warrenton Turnpike they found two undefended fords, Sudley Ford and Poplar (Red House) Ford. Barnard reported his findings, and McDowell adopted a new battle plan for Sunday, July 21:

1. A false attack [was] to be made by Richardson's brigade...on Blackburn's Ford.

2. Tyler's division [was] to move from its camp at 3 a.m. (the 21st) towards the stone bridge of the Warrenton turnpike, to feign the main attack upon this point.

3. The divisions of Hunter and Heintzelman (in the order named) [were] to leave their camps at 2:30 a.m. (they were encamped about two or three miles behind Tyler), and, following his movement, to diverge from the Warrenton turnpike at the by-road beyond Cub Run, and take the road for Sudley Springs; or, rather, it was provided...that Hunter's division should proceed to Sudley Springs, and Heintzelman to take the lower ford...[1]

4. The Fifth Division (Miles') [was] to be in reserve on the Centreville ridge.[2]

(See map 8.)

MAP 8

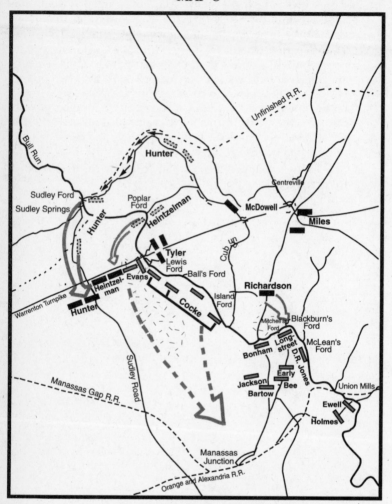

Union revised battle plan.

The main assault would be directed against the Confederate left flank. Two Union Divisions, 13,000 men, were designated to march around the Confederate left, cross Sudley Ford and Poplar Ford, and smash the Confederate left flank. Meanwhile, Tyler's and Richardson's forces were to feign attacks along their fronts.

CONFEDERATE BATTLE PLANS

On the morning of July 18, 1:00 a.m., President Davis sent Johnston a telegram stating that the Union army was closing in on Manassas, and "if practicable" would he reinforce Beauregard's army. Johnston immediately began marching toward Piedmont Station on the Manassas Gap railroad, east of the Blue Ridge mountains. (Union Major General Patterson was to have prevented Johnston's army from leaving the Shenandoah Valley. In fact, Patterson, on July 18, reported that Johnston had not left the valley.)

The first reinforcements began their thirty-mile train ride from Piedmont Station to Manassas on the nineteenth. Brigadier General Thomas Jackson's brigade arrived first. By the twentieth two more Confederate brigades, along with Johnston, joined Beauregard's army—an additional 6,000 men. Now they mustered 27,833 men and 49 cannon and were stationed accordingly along the southern bank of Bull Run.[3]

In spite of reports that McDowell's army numbered 55,000 men and was only four miles away near Centreville, Virginia, Beauregard and Johnston, at 5:00 a.m., July 21, quickly formed an offensive plan designed to turn the Union left flank.

1. Brigadier General Richard Ewell's and Brigadier General Theophilus Holmes' brigades would lead the attack on the Union left flank, crossing at Union Mills Ford.

2. At McLean's Ford, Brigadier General David R. Jones', Colonel Jubal Early's, Brigadier General Barnard Bee's, and Colonel Francis Bartow's brigades would cross and also strike the Union left flank.

3. Brigadier General James Longstreet's and Brigadier General Thomas Jackson's brigades would quickly follow the assaulting column—crossing at Blackburn's Ford.

4. The remaining Confederate brigades (Brigadier General Milledge L. Bonham's, Colonel P. St. George Cocke's and Colonel Nathaniel Evans') would strike the Union center and right flank (see map 9).[4]

To maintain an echelon attack (a tiered, continuous forward motion) the subordinate commanders were ordered to keep in close communications with each other. If all went according to plan, the Union army would be cut off from Washington, D.C., and captured by 12 noon, July 21.[5] The war would be over and Beauregard the hero.

MAP 9

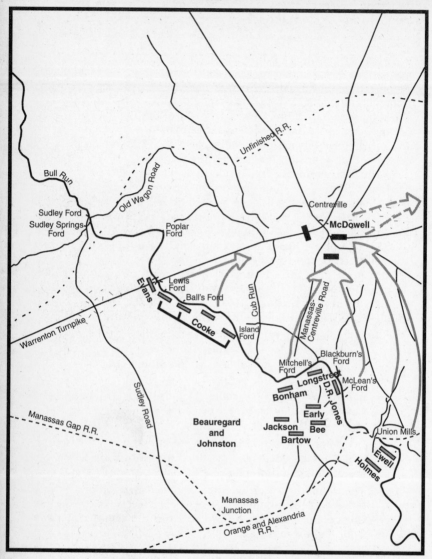

Confederates plan an offensive attack.

Coincidently, Beauregard and Johnston concentrate their assault on the Union left flank. At dawn, July 21, Ewell is ordered to launch the strike; the remaining Confederate brigades are to closely follow. The plan: to completely rout McDowell's force and open the road to Washington, D.C.

Chapter 4

STONE BRIDGE

FIRST STAGE (2:30 A.M.–8:00 A.M.)
"Fire!"

OPPOSING COMMANDERS

CONFEDERATE	UNION
Brigade Commander:	Division Commander:

Colonel Nathan G. Evans
1,100*

Brigadier General Daniel Tyler
7,512

Brigade Commanders:

---

*The 4th South Carolina (700 men), com-
manded by Colonel J.B.E. Sloan, and Major
Chatham Roberdeau Wheat's First Special
Battalion Louisiana (400) comprised Evans'
brigade.

Colonel William T. Sherman
4,452
(Seen in his brigadier general's uniform)

UNION *(cont.)*

Brigade Commanders:

Brigadier General Robert C. Schenck
3,060
(Seen in his major general's uniform)

At 2:30 a.m., July 21, two Union brigades in Tyler's division moved out of Centreville and down the Warrenton Pike toward the Stone Bridge. In order to coordinate the attack, Tyler would have to move quickly past Cub Run, allowing the main flanking force (Hunter's and Heintzelman's divisions, 13,000 men) to turn off the Warrenton Pike and head in a northwesterly direction toward Sudley Ford (about 8 miles away). McDowell estimated his flanking divisions would be in position by 7:00 a.m.

From the start, however, the Union army encountered delay. Without cavalry, not knowing exactly where the enemy was, and with no knowledge of the countryside, Tyler moved cautiously toward the Stone Bridge. By 3:00 a.m. Brigadier General Robert Schenck of Tyler's division sent out skirmishers from the 2d Ohio. Nervously and slowly the Ohioans approached the Stone Bridge.

Their commander, Captain George M. Finch, described the scene:

> *My company was deployed as skirmishers on the left of the road. We scrambled along through the dense woods and thickets, the darkness so intense that, literally, you could not see your hand before your face. We had to feel our way, keeping up our alignment at right angles with the road, as best we could, by the voice of the next man on the right. We never knew where a fence or a tree was located in front of us, until we ran slap against it. Many of the skirmishers had bloody noses and bruised limbs from such collisions.*[1]

As the 2d Ohio reached the edge of the woods they engaged the Confederates on the north bank of Bull Run. The Confederate skirmishers, however, did not resist and quickly retreated across the creek.

Finally, by 5:30 a.m., Tyler's division cleared Cub Run, and the two other divisions began their flank march toward Sudley Ford. It had taken Tyler's division (three brigades) four hours to march three miles. Between 5:15 and 6:00 a.m. his brigades deployed in the woods east of Stone Bridge. Captain J.H. Carlisle's 2d U.S. Artillery, Company E, unlimbered his four cannon in a field adjoining the road and waited for the signal gun.

Approximately one mile from the bridge, Union Lieutenant Peter C. Hains ordered the 30-pounder Parrott to fire three shots in rapid succession (see map 10). The three shots signified the opening of the first major battle of the Civil War. It was 6:00 a.m.

MAP 10

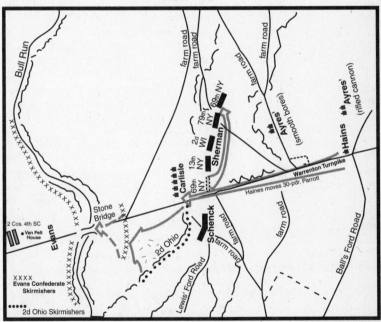

Stone Bridge

At 6:00 a.m. Lieutenant Hains fires the first shot of the engagement; it flies harmlessly over the Confederate infantrymen and strikes Mr. Van Pelt's house. Captain Carlisle's four cannon begin firing. Hains then moves the 30-pounder Parrott near Carlisle's guns while Schenck's and Sherman's brigades continue to skirmish with Evans' Confederates.

VIGNETTE:
THE 30-POUNDER PARROTT CANNON
"President Lincoln's Baby-waker"

Nineteen-year-old Lieutenant Peter C. Hains graduated from West Point on June 24, 1861. Upon graduation he was assigned to train an eleven-man crew to serve a huge 30-pounder Parrott rifled cannon. It weighed 6,000 pounds and hurled a thirty-three-pound projectile. The men, awed by its size and power, believed the Confederates would run after one shot from their beloved cannon. Hains witnessed members of his crew pat its breech and affectionately say, "Good old boy, you'll make 'em sit up—just wait a bit." As the Union army moved toward Manassas, Hains and his crew accompanied the long procession. With only ten horses and eleven men, 250 infantrymen were needed to help pull the mammoth cannon up the Virginia hills. These infantrymen, primarily from the 2d Wisconsin, nicknamed the gun "President Lincoln's Baby-waker."

The loudest of the cannon, the Baby-waker had the honor of firing the first signal shots. The cannoneers unlimbered it ½ mile east of the Stone Bridge on the Warrenton Turnpike. Shortly after 6:00 a.m. on Sunday, July 21, Hains was given the order to fire. Hains recalled, "I sighted the rifle carefully, and the men grinned their delight. Then I stood back. 'Fire!' came the order." Hains aimed at Mr. Van Pelt's house less than a mile away. The shell struck the house and the first battle of Manassas began.

As the battle progressed, Hains saw glimpses of Confederate infantry on the western side of Stone Bridge. Occasionally, his artillerymen lobbed shells into them but, because of the smoke and terrain, Hains could not accurately fire his cannon. Moreover, the battle shifted two to three miles away, and, since the cannon was too heavy to move, it could not be effectively employed. (The 250 temporarily assigned infantrymen had rejoined their respective regiments.)

In the late afternoon McDowell ordered Hains to leave the field and try to make it back to Centreville. Hains and his crew made a valiant attempt, reaching to within a mile-and-a-half of Centreville. Yet, they could not pull the cannon up the hill just beyond the Cub Run bridge without infantrymen to aid them. Subsequently, Hains rendered the cannon useless and abandoned the gun.[2]

Lieutenant Peter C. Hains,
age 19
*(Seen in his
lieutenant's uniform)*

To the Union artillerymen's surprise the Confederate troops did not panic and run. Instead, the Confederates' commander, Colonel Nathan G. Evans, ordered the infantrymen and artillerymen not to return fire. With only 1,100 men guarding the left flank, Evans realized that if he engaged the Union troops their commanders would calculate his strength and make a forced advance on his position. He therefore kept his men well-hidden within the foliage. Finally, when he observed the skirmishers across Bull Run, he directed three companies (two from the 4th South Carolina and one from Major Chatham Roberdeau Wheat's battalion, the Tiger Rifles) to advance and cover his entire front.[3]

For the next two hours (6:00 a.m.–8:00 a.m.) the two sides skirmished. Yet, with nearly 7,500 men available, Union commander Tyler did not push his force across the Stone Bridge and rout Evans' small brigade. According to McDowell's orders Tyler was "to threaten the passage of the bridge," not to carry and take the bridge.[4] His division's purpose was to divert attention away from the main flanking attack at Sudley Ford. He therefore deployed only two brigades in front of the bridge: Brigadier General Robert C. Schenck's on the left of the Warrenton Pike and Colonel William T. Sherman's to the right of the pike.

While the cannon and skirmishers created a lot of commotion, it was virtually a harmless duel. During this time Captain Finch noticed one mounted Union officer.

The 30-pounder Rifled Parrott weighed 6,000 pounds and hurled a thirty-three-pound projectile. (This is not the same cannon handled by Hains and his men.)

He was a dignified and stern-looking man, with fiery red hair and whiskers. Halting his command, he rode rapidly off to the right, in full view of the enemy's skirmishers, all of whom took a shot at him as he passed. While I admired his bravery, with ready assurance I condemned him for his recklessness, for was I not "the captain of a hundred men"? I remember saying to some one near me: "That man must be crazy."[5]

Finch later learned that this officer was Colonel William T. Sherman.

Meanwhile, the Union officers waited for the main flank attack which should have occurred by now; however, there was no sound of musketry from the direction of Sudley Ford. After an hour, Evans realized the considerable force in his front was a diversionary force and another was moving to turn his left flank. A semaphore message from Captain Edward P. Alexander clarified Evans' presumption, "Look out for your left. You are turned." Alexander, stationed about eight miles away on Wilcoxen's Hill, recalled the events in his memoirs:

...as well as I remember about 8:30 a.m., suddenly a little flash of light in the same field of view but far beyond them caught my eye. I was looking to the west and the sun was low in the east, and this flash was the reflection of the sun from a brass cannon in McDowell's flanking column approaching Sudley Ford. It was about 8 miles from me in an air line and was but a faint gleam, indescribably quick, but I had a fine glass and well trained eyes, and I knew at once what it was. *And careful ob-*

servation also detected the glitter of bayonets all along a road crossing the valley, and I felt sure that I was "on to" McDowell's plan and saw what was the best part of his army... First I signalled to Evans as of most immediate consequence, *"Look out for your left. You are flanked."* [He then quickly wrote a note to Beauregard.] *"I see a column crossing Bull Run about 2 miles above Stone Bridge. Head of it is in woods on this side; tail of it in woods on other side. About a quarter of a mile length of column visible in the opening. Artillery forms part of it."*[6] (See map 11.)

Captain Edward P. Alexander, age 26
(Seen here in his colonel's uniform)

Evans reacted quickly and boldly to this new threat. He directed Major Wheat's Louisiana Battalion and six companies of the 4th South Carolina to Matthews Hill in order to meet the Union troops. In all, Evans sent 900 men, one troop of cavalry, and two cannon to combat 13,000 Union troops. Only four companies (200 men) now guarded the Stone Bridge.

MAP 11

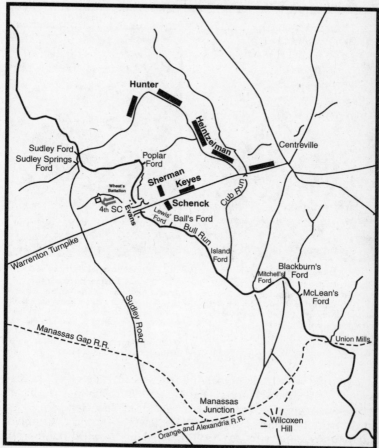

To Matthews Hill

About eight miles away, on Wilcoxen's Hill, Confederate Captain Edward Alexander signals (using semiphore) Evans that his left flank is about to be turned. Evans quickly sends Wheat's Louisiana Battalion and part of the 4th South Carolina to meet this new threat near Matthews Hill.

Chapter 5

HUNTER'S AND HEINTZELMAN'S
FLANK MARCH

> **(5:30–9:00 A.M.)**
> *"What a toilsome march it was..."*

Colonel David Hunter
Second Division Commander
Wounded in the neck during the battle on
Matthews Hill; he survived his injury. Colo-
nel Andrew Porter replaced him as the Sec-
ond Division commander.

Colonel Samuel Heintzelman
Third Division Commander
Around 2:30 p.m., while leading his division toward Henry Hill, a bullet struck him
in the arm. He refused, however, to leave
the field. Dr. William S. King, medical director of the Union army, met him on the
field and extracted the bullet while
Heintzelman sat on his horse.[1]

Around 5:30 a.m. Colonel Ambrose E. Burnside's brigade, lead
unit of Colonel David Hunter's flanking column, finally crossed Cub
Run. Four regiments formed his brigade: 2d New Hampshire, 1st
and 2d Rhode Island and the 71st New York Militia. Chaplain
Augustus Woodbury, of the 1st Rhode Island, recalled the march:

> *What a toilsome march it was through the woods! What*
> *wearisome work in clearing away the fallen trees, which*

now and then obstructed the path! The Second Regiment led the van, with skirmishers well thrown out on either side. The artillery could be moved but with difficulty...Other vehicles were along, with civilians, who wished to see the battle. The march was necessarily slow...[2]

Private Elisha Hunt Rhodes, in the 2d Rhode Island, also remembered the arduous trek:

About two o'clock this morning we left "Bush Camp," and marching down the hill, through Centreville, found the woods obstructed by wagons and troops that had failed to start on time. Soon the Second left the main road and struck off to the right, through a wood path that had been much obstructed. As we led the Brigade the task of clearing the road fell to us, and hard work we found it. About nine o'clock in the forenoon we reached Sudley church, and a distant gun startled us, but we did not realize that our first battle was so near at hand. We now took a side road that skirted a piece of woods and marched for some distance, the men amusing themselves with laughter and jokes, with occasional stops for berries.[3]

While the 2d Rhode Island cleared the road the following regiments reflected on the beauty of that Sunday morning. Lieutenant Colonel Francis S. Fiske, 2d New Hampshire, wrote:

I wish I could adequately describe the loveliness of this summer Sabbath morning. In the midst of war we were in peace. There was not a cloud in the sky; a gentle breeze rustled the foliage over our heads, mingling its murmurs with the soft notes of the wood-birds; the thick carpet of leaves under our feet deadened the sound of the artillery wheels and of the tramp of men. Everybody felt the influence of the scene, and the men, marching on their leafy path, spoke in subdued tones. A Rhode Island officer riding beside me quoted some lines from Wordsworth fitting the morning, which I am sorry I cannot recall. Colonel Slocum of the Second Rhode Island rode up and joined in our talk about the peaceful aspect of nature around us. In less than an hour I saw him killed while cheering on his men. At the door of a log hovel stood a woman who so loved the "sacred soil" that she bore much of it on her person; she told us that there were enough Confederates on ahead to wipe us all out, and that her old man

*was one of them... [Cannon fire in the distance spoiled
the peaceful moment.]...Men ceased speaking and without orders closed their ranks, and only the sullen rumble of
the artillery wheels was to be heard; the influence of our
peaceful surroundings was gone, and men were reminded
that the time which was to test their manhood had come.*[4]

Colonel Samuel Heintzelman's division slowly followed behind
Hunter's brigades.

**Chaplain
Augustus Woodbury**
1st Rhode Island

**Private
Elisha H. Rhodes**
2d Rhode Island
Throughout the war Rhodes
was promoted in rank, and
eventually became the colonel of 2d Rhode Island.
*(Seen here in his
colonel's uniform)*

**Lieutenant Colonel
Francis S. Fiske**
2d New Hampshire

Sudley Ford

It took Burnside's brigade seven-and-a-half hours (2:00 a.m.–
9:30 a.m) of tedious, tiresome trudging to reach Sudley Ford. The
flanking column was now hours behind schedule (McDowell had
hoped to attack the Confederate left flank at 7:00 a.m.). Exhausted,
thirsty and hot, Burnside allowed his men to rest and fill their canteens. Many jumped into the stream to cool themselves. Approximately half-an-hour passed before they continued their march.

After crossing Bull Run they turned sharply southward down
the Manassas-Sudley Road. At Sudley Springs Ford they crossed
Catharpin Run and an unfinished railroad grade, passing Sudley
Church and continuing into a wooded area (see map 12). The church
would soon be used as a field hospital.[5] Back at Sudley Ford,

McDowell, frustrated by the slow progress, rode up to Burnside. Clouds of dust could be seen coming towards Burnside's brigade, and McDowell's staff officers shouted to the regimental commanders, "Tell him [the colonel] to have his men ready, for we shall soon meet the enemy in large force."[6] The lead regiment, the 2d Rhode Island, was therefore sent ahead to Matthews Hill.

MAP 12

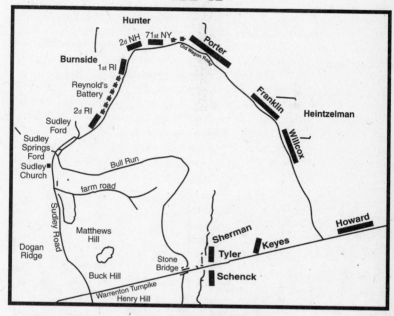

Union Flank March

Around 9:30 a.m. Colonel Ambrose Burnside's lead brigade crosses Bull Run near Sudley Ford.

Chapter 6

MATTHEWS HILL

Edgar and Martin Matthew lived in a small house at the top of the ridge. About a quarter of a mile south, Henry and Jane Matthew resided in the Stone House at the intersection of Sudley Road and the Warrenton Turnpike.

The battle for Matthews Hill included at least five stages and lasted for an hour-and-a half (10:10 a.m.–11:40 a.m.). During this time sixteen regiments (ten Union and six Confederate) clashed on this hill; nearly 1,054 were killed or wounded from the Matthews House to the Stone House.[1] Since Burnside's brigade fought only on Matthews Hill his casualties are considered in this section. Porter's brigade casualties are counted in the Young's Branch area and on Henry Hill. Although the Confederate regiments—Evans' (Wheat's battalion and 4th South Carolina), Bee's (4th Alabama, 2d and 11th Mississippi), Bartow's and 8th Georgia)—battled on Henry Hill, their heaviest losses were on Matthews Hill and Young's Branch area. Consequently, their casualty list is figured for Matthews Hill.

Matthews House, March 1862   **Stone House, March 1862**

During and after the battle soldiers used both houses as field hospitals.

FIRST STAGE (10:00 A.M.–10:30 A.M.)
"...a perfect hail storm of bullets...was poured upon us..."

OPPOSING COMMANDERS

CONFEDERATE   **UNION**

Brigade Commander: Brigade Commander:

Colonel Nathan Evans
Wheat's Battalion and six companies of
the 4th South Carolina, 900

Colonel Ambrose Burnside
Only the 2d Rhode Island, 842 men, actively took part in this stage. Burnside's
brigade numbered 3,700.

Throwing off their knapsacks, the 2d Rhode Island double-
quicked to the ridge of Matthews Hill. Union Division Commander
Colonel Hunter and Colonel John S. Slocum, 2d Rhode Island, deployed the regiment in an open field left of the Sudley-Manassas
road with the Matthews House to their left. The Rhode Island skirmishers went ahead of the main body. As they approached the rail
fence the Catahoula Guerrillas, part of Wheat's battalion, fired into
them; the bullets, aimed too high, harmlessly passed over the heads
of the Union men. The Rhode Islanders returned the fire, and the
Confederate skirmishers fell back. Private Thomas M. Aldrich, an
excited, inexperienced Union artilleryman, exclaimed to his lieutenant, "They are driving in the pickets, lieutenant!"

Lieutenant William B. Weeden replied, "I am afraid they are
hard old pickets, Aldrich."

Tom then asked, "You are not afraid, are you?"

The lieutenant smiled and answered, "No, it will not do to be
afraid,..."[2]

Private Thomas M. Aldrich
Reynolds' Rhode Island Battery

Lieutenant William B. Weeden
Reynolds' Rhode Island Battery

After this minor altercation the Rhode Island skirmishers returned to the main body and Colonel Slocum shouted, "By the left flank—MARCH!" Yelling like demons they charged across the field and climbed the fence. One boy fell off the fence and broke his bayonet. The men laughed, in contradiction to the seriousness of the situation. Private Rhodes remembered:

> ...a perfect hail storm of bullets, round shot and shell was poured upon us, tearing through our ranks and scattering death and confusion everywhere; but with a yell and a roar we charged upon them driving them again into the woods with fearful loss.[3]

At 200 yards the men exchanged fire. A Confederate Catahoula Guerrilla wrote, "The balls came as thick as hail [and] grape, bomb and canister would sweep our ranks every minute."[4] To meet the 2d Rhode Island, Wheat placed his battalion in an open field, with the woods to his left.

While the infantry battled, Burnside ordered his artillery into the fray. "Forward your artillery!" he shouted to Captain William Reynolds (see map 13).

> ...[I]n an instant the battery was smashing through a rail fence on the right, the rails flying as the guns passed over them. It was a startling sight as the battery reached the hill to see men shooting at us less than two hundred yards away.[5]

MAP 13

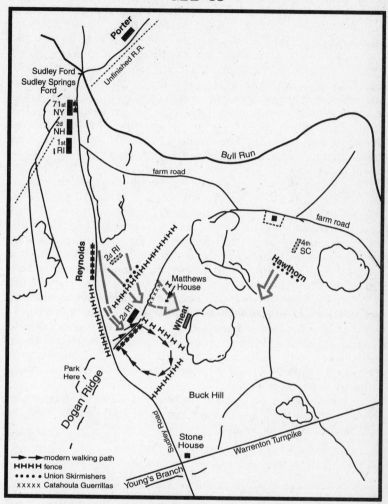

Matthews Hill • First Stage: 10:10–10:40 a.m.
The 2d Rhode Island skirmishers force the Louisiana Catahoula Guerrillas
back as the remaining troops from the 2d Rhode Island and Reynolds' Rhode
Island battery join in the fight.

As the Union artillerymen unlimbered their cannon, Colonel Hunter, their division commander, was shot through the neck and wounded. (He was taken from the field; he survived this wound. Brigade commander Colonel Andrew Porter replaced him.) Meanwhile, the artillerymen opened up with canister, case shot and shells, but the Louisiana troops stood their ground. Smoke and noise engulfed Matthews Hill, everyone firing as fast as they could load their weapons. Rhodes' smoothbore musket became so fouled that he had to strike the ramrod against a fence to force the cartridge home. Frustrated and exhausted, Rhodes picked up another weapon from the ground and threw his useless gun away. Other Rhode Islanders, desperate for protection, hid behind a haystack. This shelter was short lived; a Confederate shell exploded nearby destroying the mound. Covered with straw, the dejected men rejoined their ranks.

As Reynolds' battery deployed on the hill, the 4th South Carolina and one cannon arrived on the scene and took a position to Wheat's left. In the excitement, however, Captain Hawthorn's South Carolinian company fired into the Louisiana troops. Three men were killed and several more wounded. A few angry Louisianans shot back at the South Carolina troops. Immediately, Hawthorn and Wheat yelled at their troops, and they once again concentrated their fire on the Rhode Islanders (see map 14).

The 2d Rhode Island now began to suffer heavy casualties. Returning from reconnaissance, and in the act of climbing a fence, a bullet struck Colonel Slocum in the head. Rhodes and Private Thomas Parker carried their colonel to the Matthews' house. There they discovered the bullet had "ploughed a furrow from rear to front through the top of his head."[6] (Slocum died later at the field hospital at Sudley Church.)

Thirty minutes had passed and still the 2d Rhode Island was the only Union force engaged on Matthews Hill. Burnside finally sent in the 1st Rhode Island.

MAP 14

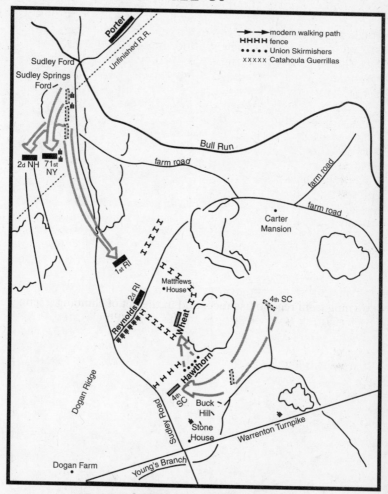

Matthews Hill • First Stage, *continued*

As skirmishers from the 4th South Carolina approach the battle they accidentally fire into Wheat's Louisiana battalion. The situation is quickly remedied
and the 4th South Carolina deploys on Wheat's left flank.

Major C. Roberdeau Wheat
1st Special Louisiana Battalion
400

Captain William H. Reynolds
Reynolds' Rhode Island Battery
6 cannon

Colonel John S. Slocum
2d Rhode Island
842

Private Elisha H. Rhodes
circa 1865

SECOND STAGE
"Lay me down, boys, you must save yourselves."

OPPOSING COMMANDERS

CONFEDERATE

Brigade Commander:

UNION

Brigade Commander:

Colonel Nathan G. Evans
Six companies from the 4th South Carolina and Wheat's battalion, 900.

Colonel Ambrose Burnside
1st and 2d Rhode Island
approximately 1,750 men.

To make room for the 1st Rhode Island, the 2d Rhode Island redeployed several yards to the left. While repositioning the 2d, an artillery shell struck Major Sullivan Ballou's leg and shattered it; he died later at a field hospital.

As they observed the 2d Rhode Island making way for the additional troops, Evans and Wheat assumed the Union regiment was falling back. Wheat's battalion, therefore, charged the cannon on the hill, coming within twenty yards of the guns. Shooting down cannoneers and horses, they swept up the slope just as the 2d was joined by the 1st Rhode Island. Both regiments threw a volley of lead into the Confederates. Demoralized, they stumbled down the hill and drifted toward the left flank of the 4th South Carolina. The effect of that action shortened the Confederate battle line. Dismounting and waving his sword above his head, Wheat desperately tried to rally his men. His display attracted Union attention as well, and a bullet drilled through his body, entering under his upstretched left arm and going through both lungs. Captain Buhoup ordered several of his Catahoula Guerrillas to carry Wheat from the field. Two of the men were shot, and Wheat painfully fell to the ground. He cried out, "Lay me down, boys, you must save yourselves."[7] The small group of Confederates began drawing a concentration of fire; yet, they were determined to carry their commander to a field hospital. The remaining Lousianans either walked to the rear or deployed to the left of the 4th South Carolina (see map 15).

It was now approaching 11:00 a.m.; at this stage more Union and Confederate units entered the fray.

Major Sullivan Ballou, age 32
A week before the battle he predicted his death in a letter to his wife, Sarah. To console her, he reassured her that they would meet again.

Major C.R. Wheat
1st Special Louisiana Battalion
Shot through both lungs; he survived his wounds.

Lieutenant Colonel Frank Wheaton
Assumed command of the 2d Rhode Island after their colonel was mortally wounded.

Major Joseph P. Balch
After a half-an-hour, Balch's 1st Rhode Island reinforced the 2d Rhode Island near Matthews house.

MAP 15

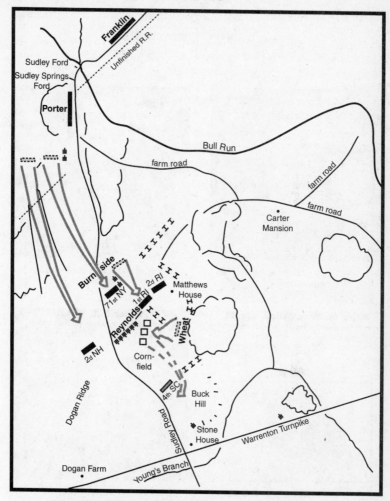

Matthews Hill • Second Stage: 10:40–10:50 a.m.

The 1st Rhode Island takes position to the right of the 2d Rhode Island. Seeing the 2d Rhode Island shifting to the left, Wheat believes they are retreating. The Louisiana battalion assaults the Union cannon and is repulsed. Wheat's men redeploy to the left of the 4th South Carolina.

THIRD STAGE
"Up Alabamians!"

OPPOSING COMMANDERS

CONFEDERATE

UNION

Brigade Commanders:

Brigade Commanders:

Brigadier General Barnard E. Bee
4th Alabama
700

Colonel Ambrose E. Burnside
3,700*

Colonel Nathan Evans
900 †

Colonel Andrew Porter
3,700
(Seen in his brigadier general's uniform)

---

* This number of men was taken into battle. The 2d Rhode Island had been fighting for half-an-hour and had already suffered heavy casualties; therefore, this number is only approximate.

†Note Evans' brigade had been involved in the first two stages and had suffered heavy casualties. In addition, the Louisiana battalion was disorganized and was not fighting as one effective unit.

Around 11:00 a.m. Porter's brigade deployed on Burnside's right flank. Evans' small band turned to meet this new threat. Finally, the first Confederate reinforcements rushed into battle. Brigadier General Barnard E. Bee ordered Colonel Egbert J. Jones' 4th Alabama down the slope of Henry Hill, across Young's Branch and up Matthews Hill. Jones deployed in the woods to the right of the 4th South Carolina. In front of the Alabama troops a field of low corn stood with a fence surrounding it. Beyond the cornfield, behind another fence, Union Captain Reynolds' six guns, two boat howitzers from the 71st New York Militia, and the Rhode Island regiments fired at the Confederates. If the Alabama regiment remained in its current position, it would be destroyed; therefore, Bee rode up to Jones and ordered the charge: "Up Alabamians!" he yelled. (Another Alabama soldier remembered distinctly hearing Bee shout: "Throw out your right and left companies as skirmishers.") Seven hundred soldiers immediately jumped up and over the fence. Men fell as they subjected themselves to the deadly fire. Under the galling musketry the Alabama officers ordered their men to lie down in the cornfield (see map 16).[8] The Confederates fired as fast as they could from a prone position, but it was a difficult task. To further complicate matters, the cornfield fronted the left of the line, and the soldiers could not see the enemy.[9] Consequently, their aim was not accurate. Colonel Jones rode up and down the line trying to encourage and steady his men. Bullets flew around him; his horse was shot, and he fell to the ground. As Jones recovered, a ball tore through both his thighs. Under the intense fire, however, his men could not carry him from the field, and he was forced to lie on the ground in agony, watching helplessly. (Egbert J. Jones died from his wounds on September 3, 1861.) Besides Jones, Captain Lewis E. Lindsay, Company K, was killed; First Lieutenant James Young assumed command of the company. The 4th Alabama's lieutenant colonel, Evander Law, and major, Charles Scott, suffered wounds as well. A shot broke Law's arm and Major Scott was wounded in the right leg.[10] Yet, in the midst of such chaos, a private in the 4th Alabama recalled laughter within their ranks.

> Although the conflict was a severe one, and the lives of the men exposed almost every moment; still, in the midst of the storm of death...many an amusing occurrence transpired which for the time being was a source of amusement and fun for the boys. Occasionally a piece of bomb would topple one of the boys topsy turvy without doing any serious damage; a minie ball would come whizzing

MAP 16

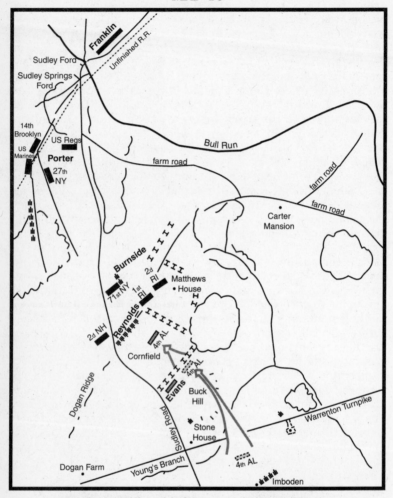

Matthews Hill • Third Stage: 10:50–11:00 a.m.
Confederate Brigadier General Bee orders the 4th Alabama to Matthews Hill.
The 4th Alabama charges the Rhode Island battery and are pinned down in the
cornfield.

*and knock a hole in some fellow's canteen letting out his
water, or tear open his haversack and spoil his dinner.
These...would cause roars of laughter.*[11]

Fighting alongside these Alabamians was a civilian named Dr.
Watkins Vaughan.

Colonel Egbert Jones, age 41
Fairly tall, at six feet three inches, Jones
graduated from the University of Virginia.
Prior to the war he practiced law and served
on the Alabama Legislature. While commanding the 4th Alabama on Matthews Hill
he was wounded in both thighs; he died
September 3, 1861.

**Lieutenant Colonel Evander Law,
age 25**
Graduated from South Carolina Military
Academy, 1856. Upon graduating he served
at the academy as assistant professor of
history and belles-lettres (a literary group).
From 1858–1860 he taught at Kings Mountain Military Academy; he then moved to
Tuskegee, Alabama and recruited Company
B, "Tuskegee Zouaves," 4th Alabama. During the fight a shot broke his arm. He recovered, and later became a leading Confederate general.
(Seen here in his general's uniform)

Captain Lewis E. Lindsay, age 41
Farmer, elected captain of Company K, 4th
Alabama, April 27, 1861; killed July 21,
1861.

Lieutenant James H. Young, age 36
Mechanic from Larkinsville, Alabama. Assumed command of Company K, 4th Alabama, after Lindsay's death. Resigned at
his one-year term of service.[12]

VIGNETTE:
DR. WATKINS VAUGHAN AND HIS PERSONAL SERVANT

While Dr. Watkins Vaughan was visiting his sons, Turner and Plutarch, the 4th Alabama was ordered into battle. Not wanting to miss the fight, Dr. Vaughan found a musket and joined the troops. His body servant, James Jefferson "Jim Jeff," decided to fight alongside his master. Plutarch's personal servant ran into the fray and tried to pull his master away, shouting, "Marster, don you know, your Ma don want you in all this here noise and confusion?"[13] His servant then ran off and left Plutarch on the field. Jim Jeff, however, remained.

After the contest, some Alabama officers shook Jim's hand and exclaimed he was a good soldier. Jefferson Davis even patted Jim on the back and told him, "You are a good true man."[14] After the war, Turner Vaughan pensioned Jim Jeff for his services to the Confederacy.

Dr. Watkins Vaughan   **James Jefferson "Jim Jeff"**

FOURTH STAGE
"This is unfair..."

OPPOSING COMMANDERS

CONFEDERATE	UNION
Brigade Commanders:	Brigade Commanders:

Brigadier General Barnard Bee

Colonel Ambrose Burnside
3,700

Colonel Francis Bartow
2,000*

Colonel Andrew Porter
3,700

Colonel Nathan Evans
900

*Bee's and Bartow's four regiments deployed from right to left: 8th Georgia, Lieutenant Colonel William Gardner; 4th Alabama, Colonel Egbert Jones; 11th Mississippi (2 companies—A & F), Lieutenant Colonel P.F. Liddell; 2d Mississippi, Colonel W.C. Falkner. See map 17. They numbered approximately 2,000 muskets. Bartow's other Georgia regiment, the 7th, did not fight on Matthews Hill.[15]

CONFEDERATE *(cont.)*

**Lieutenant Colonel
William M. Gardner, age 37**
8th Georgia
West Point graduate, 1846. A musket ball
broke his ankle; he survived his wound.
(Seen in his brigadier general's uniform)

While the first stages of Matthews Hill ensued, the 2d and 11th Mississippi and 7th and 8th Georgia waited on Henry Hill, about one half mile south. There, they came under Union artillery fire for the first time. Private Berrien McPherson Zettler, 8th Georgia (the same Georgian who had been eager to teach the abolitionists a lesson) clearly remembered the first shots.

> *I heard a cannon, and a moment after I heard the shrieking ball,—conical shell, I afterward learned it was,—and it seemed coming straight for me. The boys dropped from the apple tree like shot bears, and scrambled on hands and knees for their places in the line. Under some circumstances the sight was a laughable one, but not so to me at that moment. I felt that I was in the presence of death. My first thought was, "This is unfair; somebody is to blame for getting us all killed. I didn't come out here to fight this way; I wish the earth would crack open and let me drop in"....To say I was frightened, is tame. The truth is, there is no word in Webster's Unabridged that describes my feelings. I had never been in the very presence of death before, and if my hair at that moment had turned as white as cotton it would not have surprised me. [Their colonel, W.M. Gardner, then said:] "That went a hundred feet over us, but the next will come closer. Here it comes! lie low!" I [Private Zettler] wriggled to get lower as he directed, but the ground was hard and I couldn't get into it. I think I*

*tried to spread and flatten myself. But it was all in vain.
The noise of the ball left no room for doubt that in a moment
I would be killed. "What a fool! I'm gone! I'm dead!" Just
then the ball struck the ground a few feet ahead of us.*[16]

Their brigade commander, Colonel Francis Bartow, rode up to Lieutenant Colonel William Gardner, and shouted, "They have your range,
Colonel, charge them!" Gardner, in turn, bellowed, "Attention, right
face, double quick, march!"[17] Seven hundred Georgians jumped up
and charged across Young's Branch and up Matthews Hill.

Bee, meanwhile, saw that the 4th Alabama was overwhelmed
and in need of reinforcements. The 2d Mississippi and two companies from the 11th Mississippi joined their comrades on the
hill. Now, approximately 3,600 Confederates battled 7,400 Union
troops.

As Confederate reinforcements arrived, Burnside's two remaining Union regiments (2d New Hampshire and 71st New York Militia) deployed near Reynolds' battery (see map 17). The 2d New
Hampshire's colonel, Gilman Marston, fell with a ball through his
shoulder. Several New Hampshire men helped the cursing colonel
to the rear, and Lieutenant Colonel Francis S. Fiske assumed command of the regiment. During the fighting Fiske witnessed a shell
strike between a soldier's feet.

*...he seemed to me to rise a musket length in the air with-
out any will or effort of his own, and I expected to see him
fall dead, but he alighted on his feet with an oath, which*

Colonel	**Lieutenant Colonel**	**Colonel**
Gilman Marston	**Francis Fiske**	**Henry P. Martin**
2d New Hampshire	Assumed command of the 2d	71st New York Militia
Shot through the shoulder;	New Hampshire after Colonel	
survived his wound.	Marston was wounded.	

MAP 17

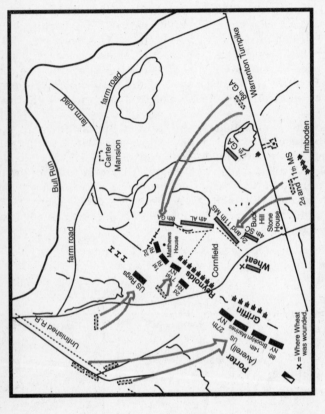

Matthews Hill • Fourth Stage: 11:05–11:15 a.m.
Confederate reinforcements arrive and threaten Burnside's left flank. Meanwhile, Burnside's remaining regiments and Porter's brigade join in the battle.

showed that he was very much alive and in no fear of immediate judgment. He walked back to Washington that night.[18]

While the 2d New Hampshire and 71st New York Militia battled around Reynolds' battery, the 1st Rhode Island, commanded by Major Joseph Balch, and the 2d Rhode Island, led now by Lieutenant Colonel Frank Wheaton, fought in the Matthews' front yard. Bearing the fire of the Rhode Islanders was the 8th Georgia.

Once on Matthews Hill, Private Zettler recalled what the Georgians saw:

...looking up the hillside, we saw the "Bluecoats" literally covering the earth. They were in the shrubbery in the front yard, down through the horse lot, behind the stables and barns and haystacks. Seemingly a thousand rifles were flashing and the air was alive with whistling bullets. Men were dropping at my right and left. I kneeled at a sapling, fired, reloaded, and fired again; but it was impossible to see if my shots hit anyone. To my right and left I could hear the balls striking our boys, and I saw many of them fall forward, some groaning in agony, others dropping dead without a word. It seemed to me, every second, a bullet cut the bark of my sapling and I felt sure I would be struck, but I loaded and fired as rapidly as I could.[19]

Major Joseph P. Balch
1st Rhode Island

Lieutenant Colonel Frank Wheaton
2d Rhode Island

Zettler saw his lieutenant colonel go down; a musket ball had broken Gardner's ankle. The private asked his colonel if he needed help; Gardner replied, "No, shoot on."[20]

As the cannon and rifle fire increased, the Rhode Island men took cover among Matthew's farmhouses. Some dropped to the ground and fired from a prone position. A Union soldier felt something between his legs and discovered one of his comrades using his legs as a port hole. Another Rhode Islander almost fainted when he simultaneously witnessed his friend fall, an artillery shell decapitate another, and a leg ripped from yet a third comrade. Blood splattered everywhere, and men became sickened; the sight was incomprehensible.[21]

Burnside realized his Rhode Island regiments could no longer hold the 8th Georgia; therefore, he sent for Major George Sykes' Regular Army infantry battalion.

FIFTH STAGE
"...for God's sake let me have the regulars."

OPPOSING COMMANDERS

CONFEDERATE   **UNION**

Colonel Nathan Evans   **Colonel Andrew Porter***
900   3,700

Brigadier General Barnard Bee

Colonel Francis Bartow†   **Colonel Ambrose Burnside**
                                           3,700

*Colonel Porter took Hunter's place as the division commander and Captain William Averell assumed command of Porter's brigade.

†Bee's and Bartow's force numbered approximately 2,000. The Confederates numbered 2,900; Union 7,400.

Tearing up on his foaming charger, Burnside excitedly demanded of Porter, "...for God's sake let me have the regulars. My
men are all being cut to pieces."[22] (Although the 8th Georgia was
flanking his left, Burnside overreacted.) Porter responded by or-
dering Major George Sykes' Regular Infantry battalion to Burnside's
left flank.[23] Lieutenant Eugene Carter led a company in this unit.

> *As soon as we were formed, we commenced firing, and
> the rebels did not like the taste of our long range rifles.
> Our men fired badly; they were excited, and some of the
> recruits fired at the stars. There was some confusion, but
> we immediately formed line of battle and marched across
> the field in splendid order for about forty rods...As we got
> to the edge of the wood we observed a white flag upon a
> sword, held by someone lying down. We went to the spot
> and found Colonel Jones of one of the Alabama regiments
> mortally wounded. He asked for a drink of water, which
> we gave him. He asked what we intended to do, and we
> told him to whip them. He said, "Gentlemen, you have got
> me, but a hundred thousand more await you!"*[24]

The only men in the immediate area, however, were Union troops
and more were arriving. Sorely outnumbered, hot, and exhausted,
the Confederates finally retreated to Henry Hill (see map 18). (The
8th Georgia suffered the heaviest casualties on Matthews Hill with
41 killed and 159 wounded; the 4th Alabama had the second highest casualties—40 killed and 156 wounded. On the Union side the
1st Rhode Island counted 13 killed, 39 wounded; the 2d Rhode
Island 23 killed and 49 wounded.)

Major George Sykes
U.S. Regulars
(Seen in his major general's uniform)

Lieutenant Eugene Carter
U.S. Regulars
(Seen in his West Point Cadet uniform)

MAP 18

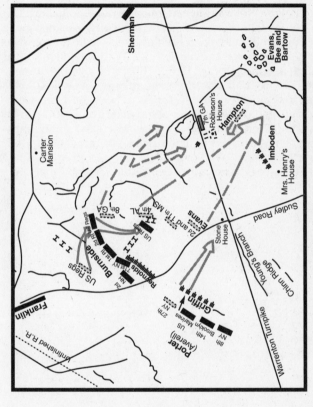

Matthews Hill • Fifth Stage: 11:15–11:30 a.m.

Major Sykes moves his U.S. Regular Infantry battalion to the left of Burnside's brigade. Outflanked and outnumbered the Confederates retreat to Henry Hill. The 27th New York charges toward the Stone House. Hampton's Legion and the 7th Georgia cover the withdrawal.

A CHANGE OF PLANS:
"The battle is there, I am going."

Although aware of McDowell's flanking column, Johnston and Beauregard assumed that three brigades (Evans', Bee's/Bartow's and Jackson's) could check this attack while the majority of the Confederate troops struck the Union left. Consequently they remained on Lookout Hill waiting for Brigadier General Richard Ewell to launch his assault. Yet, by 10:30 a.m., Ewell had not moved; Beauregard and Johnston discovered that, due to battle confusion, Ewell had never received the battle plan. With no action on their right, Johnston looked toward Henry Hill and said to Beauregard, "The battle is there, I am going."[25] Beauregard abandoned his latest strategy and quickly wrote to Ewell, Jones, and Longstreet to make only a strong demonstration along their fronts. He then sent directives to his reserve brigades (Holmes' with six cannon, Early's, and two regiments from Bonham's brigade) to move swiftly to the Confederate left flank, near Henry Hill (see map 19.)[26] Around 11:00 a.m. Johnston and Beauregard began riding toward the action.

MAP 19

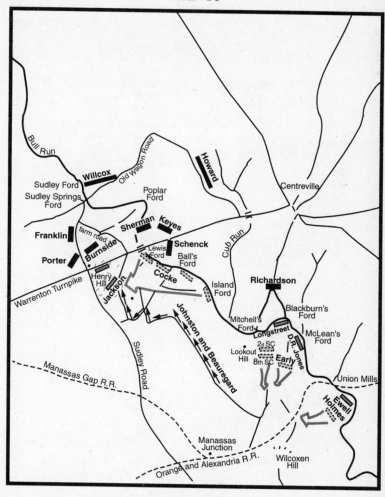

Bull Run

Willcox

Sudley Ford

Sudley Springs Ford

Old Wagon Road

Howard

Centreville

Poplar Ford

Franklin

farm road

Sherman

Keyes

Schenck

Porter

Burnside

Lewis Ford

Ball's Ford

Henry Hill

Jackson

Cocke

Island Ford

Richardson

Warrenton Turnpike

Cub Run

Sudley Road

Johnston and Beauregard

Mitchell's Ford

Blackburn's Ford

Longstreet

McLean's Ford

D.R. Jones

Lookout Hill

2d SC

8th SC

Early

Union Mills

Manassas Gap R.R.

Ewell

Holmes

Manassas Junction

Orange and Alexandria R.R.

Wilcoxen Hill

To Henry Hill

With their left flank turned, Johnston and Beauregard quickly direct their
reserve brigades to this area and begin riding toward the hill.

Chapter 7

YOUNG'S BRANCH

> **(11:30 A.M.–12:00 NOON)**
> *"Give it to them, boys!"*

OPPOSING COMMANDERS

CONFEDERATE	UNION

Regimental Commanders: Regimental Commander:

Colonel Wade Hampton
Hampton's Legion
600

Colonel Henry Warner Slocum
27th New York
667*

Colonel Lucius J. Gartrell
7th Georgia
700

---

* During the battle the 27th lost twenty-seven killed, including one officer, and forty-four wounded. In addition, sixty men were reported missing; most of them were wounded and taken prisoner. One of these prisoners was Corporal Charles Fairchild who later wrote the regiment's history. At First Manassas a spent ball from a canister shot struck him in the left breast which lodged in his shirt pocket. He was taken captive and parolled on May 22, 1862.[1]

As the Confederate commanders rode toward the action, the remnants of Evans', Bee's and Bartow's units crowded behind James Robinson's house. About 150 yards away, Confederate Captain John Imboden, with four cannon, frantically poured shot and shell into the Union ranks on Matthews Hill and John Dogan's farm.[2] Nearby, in the yard of the Robinson house, Colonel Wade Hampton's South Carolina Legion awaited orders. With the left flank crushed, Hampton and the 7th Georgia covered the Confederate retreat. South Carolinian Private John Coxe recalled the chaos:

> ...as we reached the plateau Sergeant Cleveland, of my company, was hit in the stomach with a rifle ball and fell down to the left. The ball struck the big brass buckle of his belt and made a great noise. He was badly hurt, but not fatally. The legion rushed on toward the Robinson house, head of column to the front, and as we went we met many retreating stragglers and saw our artillery still firing near the Henry house...The Warrenton Turnpike and a little stream were about a hundred yards down the hill in front, and the Federal infantry and batteries were in a field some distance beyond.
>
> We rushed down through the Robinson garden, where Private Story, of my company, was killed, and took position behind a rock wall crowned by a picket fence immediately on the Warrenton Turnpike; and here, well protected, we fired many more rounds into the enemy not far away.[3]

The Union troops vollied back; a bullet passed through the head of the legion's lieutenant colonel, Benjamin J. Johnson, killing him instantly. The legion's adjutant, Theodore J. Barker, also fell severely wounded, and Hampton's horse was killed from under him.

The Union troops which fired upon Hampton's Legion were from the 27th New York, commanded by Colonel Henry Warner Slocum (not related to Colonel John Slocum of the 2d Rhode Island). When the 27th reached the crest of John Dogan's farm they became "Excited and enraged by its casualties,"

Private John Coxe
Hampton's Legion

and charged into the valley, past the
Stone House.[4] The Confederate artillery
opened on them with canister; Private
Wesley Randall, age 25, fell dead.
Slocum dismounted and directed the
color guard to the left and rear of the
Stone House (see map 20). Noticing two
gray-clad regiments approaching from
their rear and left, the 27th mistakenly
assumed the men were from the 8th
New York, who were also dressed in
their gray militia uniforms. The 27th
watched as the soldiers fronted their
regiment; a few New Yorkers fired, but
their comrades quickly rebuked them.
Corporal Charles Bryant Fairchild witnessed the confusing scene:

Adjutant Theodore Barker
Hampton's Legion
Severely wounded near Young's
Branch; he survived his wound.

> ...a Confederate straggler between the lines, ran up to Col.
> Slocum, and declared that the "regiment yonder wanted
> to surrender." Slocum threatened the man with drawn
> sword, but he persisted; and, by the Colonel's order, Adju-
> tant Jenkins started towards the enemy, waving a have-
> lock as a flag of truce. "What regiment are you?" he asked.
> He was answered by the unfurling of the Confederate col-
> ors and the firing of a volley. He rode back to our lines,
> exclaiming, "Give it to them, boys!" The 27th responded,
> firing at will, but many did not hear him, and still held
> their fire. Our mistake had given them time to form in line
> of battle, under cover of thick bushes, and they poured
> volley after volley into us, with deadly effect. Our men
> replied vigorously, but could not long stand under such a
> fire, and began to retire slowly over the crest of the hill.
> The colors were the last to retire.[5]

Most of the New Yorkers retreated to Buck Hill and continued
to fight at a distance, while a few remained near Young's Branch. In
the withdrawal, Colonel Slocum was shot through the hip. (He survived his wound.)

On the Confederate side, stragglers from the 4th Alabama and
8th Georgia joined the South Carolina legion and 7th Georgia; the
battle intensified, and the New Yorkers' weapons became so hot
that they cooled them in the water of Young's Branch.[6]

MAP 20

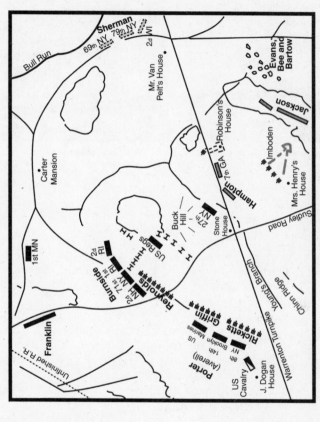

Young's Branch • 11:30–11:45 a.m.

The 27th New York battles Hampton's South Carolina Legion and the 7th Georgia. Confederate Captain Imboden pulls back his guns and redeploys southeast of Mrs. Henry's house.

Adjutant John Jenkins
27th New York

Captain William Averell
Assumed command of Porter's brigade.
*(Seen in his brigadier
general's uniform)*

Near the Henry House, Imboden's four smoothbore cannon dueled with sixteen Union rifled cannon on Dogan's farm and Matthews Hill. At this distance the rifled cannon had the advantage over Imboden's smoothbores. Low on ammunition, with half his horses killed, Imboden resolved to limber up and withdrawal (see map 22). During this time, a shell disabled one of his cannon, and he abandoned it on the field.

Observing the movement of the Confederate cannon, Captain William Averell directed the 8th New York Militia and the 14th Brooklyn to Henry Hill. Yet, when the regiments reached the Warrenton Pike, another Union officer sent them to engage Hampton's Legion. Two Confederate cannon, positioned near the Legion, fired into the New York regiments. Confused and frightened the New Yorkers quickly returned to Dogan's farm.

Although the Confederates swiftly scattered the New York regiments, Hampton's officers realized the legion was far in advance of any infantry support. Subsequently, they ordered the South Carolinians to redeploy about one-hundred yards to the rear in a small lane leading from the turnpike to the Robinson's house. The men now stood at right angles to their original line behind a flimsy, latticework fence; the fence, however, provided inadequate protection (see map 21). Private Coxe explained their situation:

...By this time we didn't care much as to what happened. Our rifle fire sounded like the popping of caps, our throats were choked with powder, and we were burning up with thirst. At length, becoming alarmed at our isolated position, Conner shouted and said: "Fall back in good order, men!" And after we got back of the Robinson house there was a lull in the noise of battle.[7]

Behind the Robinson house Evans, Bee and Bartow continued to reorganize their troops. One Confederate officer of note was Lieutenant Harry T. Buford.

MAP 21

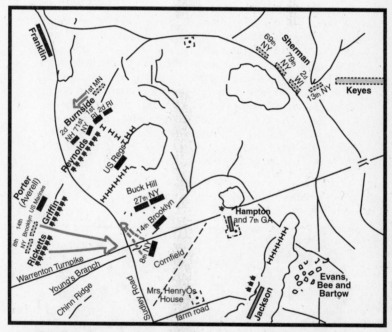

Young's Branch • Second Stage: 11:45 a.m.–12:00 p.m.
The 27th New York falls back to Buck Hill. The 8th New York and 14th Brooklyn assault Hampton's Legion and the 7th Georgia but are quickly repulsed. Near a small farm ford Sherman's brigade crosses Bull Run as Jackson's brigade arrives on Henry Hill.

VIGNETTE:
LIEUTENANT HARRY T. BUFORD

Unknown to Lieutenant Harry T. Buford's comrades his real name was Madame Loreta Janeta Velazquez. After the Mexican War the United States Government seized her father's estate. At the outbreak of the Civil War she saw an opportunity to avenge her family's dishonor and experience some adventure and excitement. She donned a male disguise and appropriated the uniform of a Confederate officer. Her first great battle was First Manassas.

Not being officially attached to a regiment, Velazquez chose to fight with Brigadier General Bee's brigade. In her memoirs she recalled her feelings during the initial conflict on Matthews Hill:

> I was wrought up to such a pitch of excitement, while the fight was going on, that I had no comprehension whatever of the value of the movements being made by the different commanders. I only saw the enemy before me, and was inspired by an eager desire to conquer him. I forgot that I was but a single figure in a great military scheme; and as, while we stood face to face with the foe, every man on the other side became for the moment my personal enemy, whom I was furious to overcome, so, when by the general's command, we were compelled to fall back, I was overcome with rage and indignation, and felt all the shame and mortification of a personal defeat.[8]

After the battle she spent time with the Louisiana men. When she realized there was no prospect for another conflict in the near future, she rode on to Richmond.

Lieutenant Harry T. Buford   **Madame Loreta Janeta Velazquez**

Chapter 8

LULL IN THE INFANTRY FIGHT

CONFEDERATES: (12:00–1:00 P.M.)
"I'll support your battery."

Captain John Imboden
(Seen here in a general's uniform)

Brigadier General Thomas Jackson
(Seen here in his lieutenant general's uniform)

The Confederates used the respite to reinforce Henry Hill. Brigadier General Thomas Jackson's Virginia brigade reached the area first about 12:00 noon. Riding at the head of his men, Jackson met Captain Imboden as he was retreating. Enraged at being left alone on the hill, Imboden, swearing, vented his frustration to Jackson. The general, however, calmly replied, "I'll support your battery. Unlimber right here."[1] Imboden unlimbered his three cannon about three-hundred yards from the Henry House on the southeastern edge of the hill. Shortly after this thirteen additional cannon arrived, previously ordered up by Johnston and Beauregard. Immediately, Jackson deployed them near Imboden's guns. Captain Imboden then limbered his cannon and went to the rear to refill his ammunition caissons while the newly arrived cannoneers continued to duel with the Union artillerymen.

After speaking with Imboden, Brigadier General Bee rode up and shouted to Jackson, "General, they are beating us back!"

Jackson replied, "Then, sir, we will give them the bayonet..."[2]

Determined to stay and fight, Jackson ordered his men to lie down behind the cannon and await reinforcements. Many of the Union artillery shells overshot the cannon and exploded near the Virginia infantry, terrifying the raw recruits. Despite the shelling, by choosing the reverse slope of Henry Hill, Jackson displayed brilliant tactical insight. Two houses stood on Henry Hill (actually a plateau): Mrs. Judith Henry's house overlooked Young's Branch and the Sudley Road-Warrenton Turnpike Intersection. About six-hundred yards northeast of her house, Mr. James Robinson, a freedman, lived in a small farmhouse. A thick wooded area lined the

MAP 22

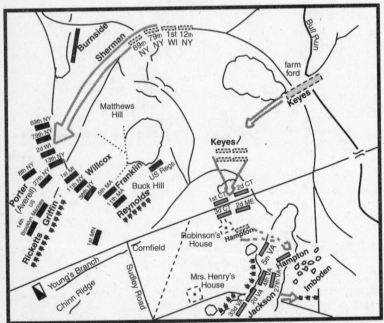

Lull in the Infantry Battle • Henry Hill • 12:30–1:30 p.m.
Sherman's brigade deploys near Porter's troops while Keyes begins his assault near the Robinson House. McDowell assembles about 18,860 men while Confederate Brigadier General Jackson's brigade (2,412) awaits another Union assault. Thirteen Confederate cannon continue to duel with the Union batteries. Captain Imboden takes his three cannon to restock the ammunition chests.

southern edge of the plateau.[3] Realizing his brigade was outnumbered (2,412),[4] Jackson hid his force in the pine thicket below the
crest of the hill (see map 22). Had he placed his brigade at the
crest of Henry Hill they would have been subject to direct artillery
and infantry fire, and their strength quickly discovered. Consequently, the Union might have pressed their attack. As it was, the
reverse slope position concealed Jackson's brigade and gave the
Virginians protection from enemy fire. If the Union infantry crested
the hill, they still had to cross three-hundred yards in an open
field before engaging the enemy within the trees, thus allowing
the Confederate artillery and infantry time to cut down any small
unit attacks.[5]

Robinson's House, circa 1862

Sudley Road, looking north, toward the Stone House, circa 1880s

Shortly after Jackson deployed his men, Johnston and Beauregard arrived at Henry Hill (about 12:00 noon). The generals decided to split their responsibilities: Beauregard took immediate command of the troops on the hill, and Johnston assumed control over the entire line, directing the rest of the reinforcements—Holmes', Bonham's, Elzey's, and Early's brigades—to Henry Hill.

Beauregard, in the meantime, rode up and down the field trying to rally the disorganized squads from Evans', Bee's and Bartow's regiments. Shells exploded around him; one disemboweled his horse. He fell hard but showed no sign of distress and quickly mounted another horse.[6] By 1:30 p.m. Beauregard calculated he had 6,500 men and thirteen pieces of artillery at his command.[7] (Beauregard seems to have considered the casualties already suffered in Evans', Bee's and Bartow's regiments when he calculated this number. In actuality, Beauregard had only Jackson's and Hampton's units ready [3,012 men]. Evans', Bee's and Bartow's units were still disorganized and had suffered heavy casualties. Reinforcements, however, rapidly marched to their aid.)

UNION
"They are running! The day is ours."

While the Confederates hurriedly established a battle line, more Union brigades reached Matthews Hill. Earlier, around 10:30 a.m., McDowell had directed Tyler to "press the attack" at Stone Bridge.[8] Tyler, however, did not relay the order to his brigade commanders until after 11:00 a.m. When the directive arrived, Colonel Sherman immediately crossed Bull Run at a small farm ford.[9] In his memoirs Sherman described the situation:

> *We found no difficulty in crossing over, and met with no opposition in ascending the steep bluff opposite with our infantry, but it was impassable to the artillery, and I sent word back to Captain Ayres to follow if possible, otherwise to use his discretion...Advancing slowly and cautiously with the head of the column, to give time for the regiments in succession to close up their ranks, we first encountered a party of the enemy* [possibly stragglers from the 4th South Carolina or Georgia troops] *retreating along a cluster of pines; Lieutenant-Colonel Haggerty, of the Sixty-ninth, without orders, rode out alone, and endeavored to intercept their retreat. One of the enemy, in full view, at short range, shot Haggerty, and he fell dead from his horse.*[10]

Captain Romeyn B. Ayres
Company E, 5th U.S. Artillery
(Seen here in his major general's uniform)

Captain James Haggerty
Acting Lieutenant Colonel, 69th New York
Shot through the heart and killed instantly.

After a short fire fight the Confederates retreated, and Sherman's brigade continued to Matthews Hill, forming behind Porter's regiments.

In the meantime, McDowell and his staff rode through the Union troops shouting, "Victory! Victory! The day is ours! They are running! They are in retreat"[11] For the moment 6,500 Confederates stood between McDowell and the Confederate rear; however, only 3,000 were battle-ready. McDowell had between 13,000–18,000 men and twenty-four cannon on hand. If he acted quickly and continued the assault he could get behind the Confederate army and completely rout the remaining brigades (see map 22). Though the soldiers awaited the order to pursue, McDowell did not press the advantage. He assumed the Confederates were completely demoralized, and his victory could be taken at any time, a conjecture which would cost him the day.[12]

Chapter 9

THE BATTLE FOR HENRY HILL

From 1:30–4:00 p.m. chaos reigned on Henry Hill. For purposes of explication, the complex, continuous action has been divided into fifteen stages; after the second stage it is impossible to provide an accurate time. There are several reasons for the confusing nature of this contest: 1) Fifteen Union regiments and thirteen Confederate regiments charged and counterattacked so quickly that the action became a whirlpool of obscurity. 2) Afterwards, not even the participants could provide a clear account. 3) Many Union regiments fired only a few rounds before falling back; as another regiment replaced them, the retreating and charging men became intermingled. 4) As a result, several Union regiments became so disorganized that the soldiers fought in smaller, make-shift battalions. 5) Confederate units combined as well. Those that assailed Matthews Hill either joined with other regiments, battled in make-shift battalions, or rested behind the lines.

To add to the confusion, many Union regiments wore gray uniforms which created a distressing dilemma for Confederate and Union alike. The similarity of flags also contributed to officers mistaking enemy regiments for their own. Frequently one could hear, "Stop firing; you are shooting at your friends."

ROBINSON HOUSE • (1:30 P.M.–2:00 P.M.)
"...the fire became so hot...it...
would have annihilated my whole line."

OPPOSING COMMANDERS

| CONFEDERATE | UNION |

Private John N. Opie, age 17*
Company L, "West Augusta Guards,"
5th Virginia
380

Colonel Charles D. Jameson
2d Maine†
772

Colonel Wade Hampton
Hampton's Legion
600

Colonel John L. Chatfield
3d Connecticut
789‡

---

*Colonel Kenton Harper commanded the 5th Virginia during the battle. Since his photo is un-
available, Opie will represent the 5th Virginia. After the battle Opie enrolled at Virginia Military
Institute; he is pictured here in his cadet uniform.

†The 2d Maine fronted the 5th Virginia and Hampton's Legion; the 3d Connecticut deployed to
the 2d Maine's right flank.

‡In this fight approximately 980 Confederates battled 1,552 Union troops.

CONFEDERATE *(cont.)*   **UNION** *(cont.)*

Colonel Erasmus Keyes
Commander of the First Brigade, Tyler's division.

Brigadier General Daniel Tyler
Commander of the First Division McDowell's army.

After Sherman's brigade crossed Bull Run, Colonel Erasmus Keyes' brigade followed. Brigadier General Tyler, their division commander, however, ordered Keyes to "take a battery on a height in front."[1] Keyes therefore directed two of his regiments, the 2d Maine and 3d Connecticut, to press the attack on Henry Hill.

Having left their coats and knapsacks on the east side of Bull Run, the New Englanders ran down the slopes and across Young's Branch (½ mile). Exhausted and hot, the men stopped at the Warrenton Turnpike and quickly deployed—the 3d Connecticut on the right and the 2d Maine on the left.[2]

At the center of the Maine line, Color Sergeant William S. Deane unfurled the regimental colors, nicknamed the "California flag." Women from Maine, now living in San Francisco, had made the flag and sent it home to their boys.[3] With the flag uncased, Colonel Jameson led the 2d Maine forward. Only advancing one-hundred yards, Keyes directed the two regiments to lie down and load their weapons. The New Englanders loaded their smoothbore muskets with .69 caliber buck and ball, and yelling like demons, rushed up the hill. (A Confederate later described the "Yankee" yell as sounding like "Hoo-ray! Hoo-ray! Hoo-ray!" The first sound "hoo," if heard at all, was a short, low, indistinct tone; "Ray," a high, long tone, slightly deflected at the end. Many times it sounded like "heigh-ray!")[4]

Nearly surrounded, Hampton's Legion fell back. The 5th Virginia and 2d Maine, both in gray uniforms, hesitated. The 5th then fired, but without the support of Hampton's Legion, they retreated and redeployed in a small wooded area, about one-hundred yards south of the Robinson house. Using the trees as cover, the 5th sent a devastating fire into the Union regiments.[5]

Near the Robinson House, the 2d Maine and 3d Connecticut lay down behind the fence previously occupied by the Confederates. Their old smoothbores became hot and fouled with black powder, but they continued to frantically load and fire. Men swore, mad with rage and zeal; yet, with only a small fence protecting them, the casualties mounted. A bullet passed through Color Sergeant Deane's throat, and he quickly bled to death; Captain Elisha N. Jones fell paralyzed, his spine broken when a bullet drove through his body. He later died from this wound.

Keyes remembered: "the fire became so hot that an exposure to it of five minutes would have annihilated my whole line";[6] however, instead of supporting the 2d Maine and 3d Connecticut with his other two regiments, Keyes and Tyler ordered the men to fall back to the Warrenton Turnpike. Under Tyler's guidance, Keyes moved his entire brigade by the left flank (see map 23). Due to the confusion, poor communication and generalship, Keyes' attack did not coordinate with McDowell's assault on Henry Hill, and for the remainder of the day Keyes' brigade stood idle, virtually behind the Confederate right flank.

(The 2d Maine lost 37 killed and wounded with 118 missing; the 3d Connecticut suffered 17 killed and wounded, 18 missing.)

MAP 23

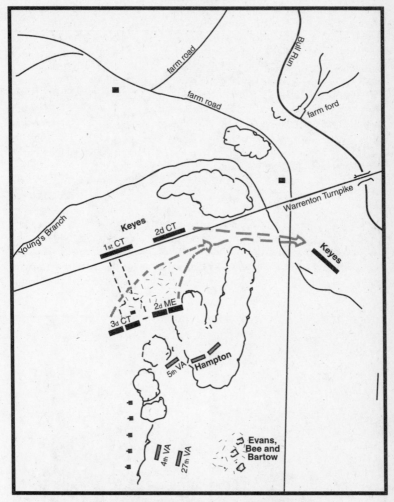

Henry Hill • First Stage: 1:30–2:00 p.m.

A close-up view of the 3rd Connecticut and 2d Maine's attack. Hampton's Legion and the 7th Georgia are forced back, but the 5th Virginia repositions in the pine thicket and sends a devasting fire into the New Englanders. Keyes then retreats and redeploys. His brigade is essentially behind the Confederate line. Yet, out of touch with McDowell, his brigade stands idle throughout the remainder of the battle.

An engraving of Robinson's House, looking north, as the Confederates viewed it

Color Sergeant
William S. Deane, age 36
Shot in the neck, KIA.

Captain Elisha N. Jones, age 39
Company C, "Brewer Artillery," from
Orrington, Maine. Shot in the back and
mortally wounded.

SECOND STAGE* • (1:45–2:15 P.M.)
"...mark my words, they will not support us."

UNION ARTILLERY OFFICERS

Major William Barry, age 43
McDowell's Chief of Artillery
(Seen in his brigadier general's uniform)

Captain Charles Griffin, age 36
Company D, 5th U.S. Artillery (5 guns)

Captain James B. Ricketts, age 44
Company I, 1st U.S. Artillery (6 guns)
(Seen in his brigadier general's uniform)

Lieutenant Charles Hazlett, age 23
Company D, 5th U.S. Artillery

---

* The U.S. Marine battalion (250), commanded by Colonel John G. Reynolds, also participated in the initial infantry action. The majority of recruits, however, were rookies and after the first shots they ran for cover.

MAP 24

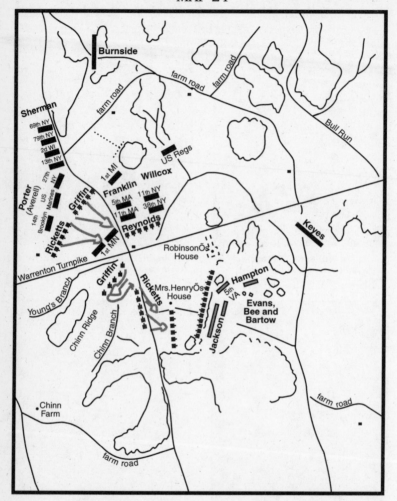

Henry Hill • Second Stage: 1:45–2:30 p.m.

Finally, after two hours, McDowell sends Captain Griffin's and Ricketts' batteries to Henry Hill. Griffin's battery gets sidetracked while Ricketts' battery unlimbers to the right of Mrs. Henry's house.

After nearly two hours of resting and reorganizing his forces, McDowell, at 1:30 p.m., told his chief of artillery, Major William F. Barry, to send two batteries to Henry Hill. Barry directed Captain Charles Griffin's and Captain James B. Ricketts' batteries forward. Both captains opposed the new position; the batteries would be in the open and too close to the Confederate infantry. In addition, they needed infantry support to protect their cannon from a Confederate assault. Major Barry assured Griffin that the Fire Zouaves (11th New York) would support the batteries. Skeptical, Griffin retorted, "I will go; but mark my words, they will not support us."[7] Griffin's five guns (one had become jammed earlier and was left on John Dogan's farm) led the way; Ricketts' six followed. The convoy moved through the valley, across Young's Branch, and down the Sudley Road. Due to a misunderstanding in directions, Lieutenant Charles E. Hazlett, on the first cannon, turned right and headed for the Chinn farm. Ricketts' battery, however, turned left into Mrs. Henry's yard, and unlimbered to the right of the house (see map 24). Ricketts recounted, "I had scarcely got into battery before I saw some of my horses fall and some of my men wounded by the sharpshooters [who were hiding in the house]. I turned my guns upon the house and literally riddled it."[8] Unknown to the Union artillerymen, Mrs. Judith Henry lay in her bed.

VIGNETTE:
MRS. JUDITH HENRY

During the mid-day lull, after several shells struck near the Henry House, Ellen and John Henry attempted to carry their elderly mother, Judith, out of her home. Their hope of safety was a farm several miles away. The battle, however, intensified around them, and they returned carrying their mother back to her bedroom. Terrified, the family cowered as the shells fell in and around the house. One shell burst directly in Judith's room, wounding her in the neck and side, and blowing off part of one foot. Her colored servant, a hired girl named Lucy Griffiths, was also wounded in the arm. Judith died later that day from her wounds.

After the battle the Confederates buried Mrs. Henry a few yards from her house. She was eighty-five years old and the only civilian killed during the battle.[9]

While Ricketts' artillery battered the Henry House, Griffin redirected his five cannon to Henry Hill and deployed them to the left of the house.[10] For over half-an-hour thirteen Confederate cannon (eleven smoothbore and two rifled), and eleven Union cannon (nine rifled and two smoothbore) dueled at less than 300 yards. Lieutenant Hazlett recalled the cannonade:

A drawing by Leon J. Fremaux of Mrs. Judith Henry's house as seen after the battle. Her house became the center of the fighting during the afternoon and was riddled by artillery and musket fire.

We had been in action there for some time; the fire was exceedingly hot; and being in such close range of the enemy we were losing a great many men and horses. We were in full relief on top of the hill, while they were a little behind the crest of the hill. We presented a better mark for them than they did for us.[11]

In addition to these complications, the Union rifled cannon, which were more effective at longer ranges, either overshot the Confederate cannon and exploded over Jackson's brigade, or the shells bored several feet into the ground and then exploded, the fragments dispersing harmlessly into the earth.

As the shells burst over the prone Virginians, men prayed, "Oh Lord! Have mercy upon me! Have mercy upon me!" And, nearby, someone cried, "Me too, Lord! Me too, Lord!"[12] To ease the men's fears, Beauregard and Jackson continued to ride up and down the line. Jackson shouted, "Steady, men! steady! all's well!"[13]

While Jackson's brigade hugged the earth, three Union infantry regiments (U.S. Marine battalion, 11th New York, and the 1st Minnesota) arrived and deployed in the rear of Griffin's and Ricketts' guns (see map 25). Two companies from the 1st Minnesota approached to within fifty to sixty yards of the Confederate line.

At first, Colonel Arthur Cummings, 33d Virginia, mistook the line for arriving Confederate reinforcements and yelled, "Cease firing, you are firing on friends!" As Cummings shouted, a volley came from the Union line; Private John Casler of the 33d sarcastically cried, "Friends, hell! That looks like it."[14]

Similar confusion occurred on the Union side. Several Minnesota men fired at the body of troops to their front. Their colonel, William A. Gorman, "Willis," exclaimed, "Stop firing—they are our friends."[15] The Confederates then answered with a volley of their own, and the Union officers ordered their men to lie down and fire. An 11th New York Zouave private recalled his experience:

...Crashing through the cornfield, singing and whistling around our ears, making the air blue and sulphurous with smoke, came a storm of bullets upon us from the woods in front. "Down, every one of you," cried the Colonel. And we went down just in time to escape the second volley. No orders came all along the line. One and then another would jump up and fire and then lie down to reload. Some started toward the woods on their own account, crawling slowly along in hopes to get sight of the foe.[16]

MAP 25

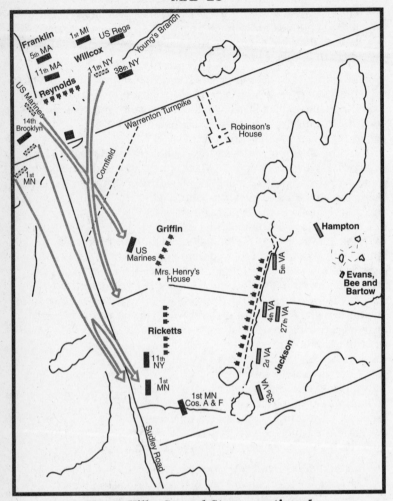

Franklin
5th MA
11th MA
1st MI US Regs
Willcox
11th NY 38th NY
Reynolds
US Marines
14th Brooklyn
1st MN

Young's Branch

Warrenton Turnpike

Robinson's House

Cornfield

Griffin
US Marines

Mrs. Henry's House

Ricketts
11th NY
1st MN

1st MN Cos. A & F

Sudley Road

Hampton

5th VA
4th VA
27th VA
2d VA
33d VA

Jackson

Evans, Bee and Bartow

Henry Hill • Second Stage, *continued*

Griffin's battery finally unlimbers to the left of Mrs. Henry's house. The U.S.
Marine battalion lies down behind Griffin's battery while the 11th New York and
1st Minnesota come up the hill to Ricketts' right. In the battle confusion two
companies from the 1st Minnesota are separated from the regiment.

One bullet struck Colonel Noah Farnham, 11th New York, in the left side of the head. (He died later in Washington, D.C.)[17]

As smoke covered the battlefield, Sergeant John G. Merritt, with several of his Minnesota comrades, ran toward the Confederate color-bearer.

> *The man who carried the colors was about five feet ten or eleven inches, dark complexioned, with black hair, slight mustache and black eyes; he with others about him wore gray clothes and black slouch hats; some one was trying to form them. The color-bearer had his coat unbuttoned, with his hat on the back of his head. As I got within a couple feet of him I commanded him in a peremptory manner to surrender, and at the same time Dudley, Durfee and myself cocked our guns. I grabbed the colors out of his hand; he and one or two more said, 'Don't shoot! don't shoot!'...As soon as I grabbed the colors out of the Johnnie's hands I told him to follow me quick, and at the same time told my men to get back to the regiment as soon as possible. Dudley, Grim and myself were laughing at the easy thing we had [done], and all of us running for the regiment as fast as we could go, when—bang! bang! bang! came a volley after us, killing Grim and the comrade whose name I have forgotten, and at the same time a dozen or more of Rebs ran after us, some of them hollering 'Kill the d——d black abolition, red-shirt Yankee,.....'[18]*

The Confederates fired again, killing Durfee and wounding Merritt in the leg. He continued to carry the flag, but the angry Confederates soon overwhelmed him. One man hit Merritt over the head with the butt of his musket and pulled the flag from his hands. The entire episode lasted only minutes.

The 11th New York and 1st Minnesota fired four to five rounds per man and then began to retreat down the hill and gather on Sudley Road—only fifteen to twenty minutes had passed.

On the Confederate side Colonel James Ewell Brown Stuart, commander of the First Virginia Cavalry, saw the retreating Union troops and mistook them for Confederates. He rode out amongst them and exclaimed, "Don't run, boys; we are here." The Union troops ignored him, and Stuart soon saw a man carrying the U.S. flag. He immediately rode back to his cavalrymen. Cutting right and left, Stuart's 150 horsemen charged into the Union troops. Virginian Lieutenant William Willis Blackford participated in the charge.

Private John Casler, age 23
Company A, "Potomac Guards"
33d Virginia
450

(Self-portrait)

Colonel William A. Gorman
1st Minnesota
900
(Seen in his brigadier general's uniform)

Colonel Noah Farnham
11th New York
900
Mortally wounded in the head; he died August 14, 1861.

Sergeant John G. Merritt
1st Minnesota
Later won the Congressional Medal of Honor for attempting to capture a Confederate flag.

Colonel Jeb Stuart, age 28   **Lieutenant William Blackford, age 30**

...when within a couple of horses's lengths of them, I leaned down, with my carbine cocked, thumb on hammer and forefinger on trigger, and fixed my eye on a tall fellow I saw would be the one my course would place in the right position for the carbine, while the man next to him, in front of the horse, I would have to leave to Comet. I then plunged the spurs into Comet's flanks and he evidently thought I wanted him to jump over this strange looking wall I was riding him at, for he rose to make the leap; but he was too close and going too fast to rise higher than the breast of the man, and he struck him full on the chest, rolling him over and over under his hoofs and knocking the rear rank man to one side. As Comet rose to make the leap, I leaned down from the saddle, rammed the muzzle of the carbine into the stomach of my man and pulled the trigger. I could not help feeling a little sorry for the fellow as he lifted his handsome face to mine while he tried to get his bayonet up to meet me; but he was too slow, for the carbine blew a hole as big as my arm clear through him.[19]

Two companies of Zouaves rushed the cavalrymen with bayonets and attempted to stab their opponents. Other Union infantry scattered throughout the woods and down Sudley Road. Thinking they had routed the regiments, the Confederate cavalrymen rode back to the Confederate line (see map 26).

MAP 26

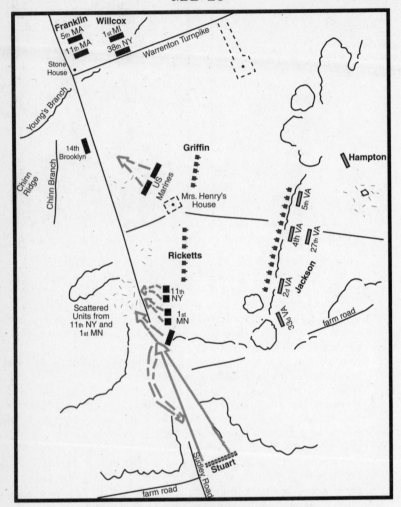

Henry Hill • Second Stage, *continued*

Confederate and Union regiments exchange musket fire; the U.S. Marines break immediately. The 11th New York and 1st Minnesota fire four or five rounds per man and retreat to Sudley Road. Confederate Colonel Jeb Stuart's Virginia cavalrymen charge into the disorganized troops. After a short melée the Virginians break off their attack.

THIRD STAGE
"Charge bayonets!"

OPPOSING COMMANDERS

CONFEDERATE   **UNION**

Private John Casler*
Company A, "Potomac Guards,"
33d Virginia
450

Captain Charles Griffin
Company D, 5th U.S. Artillery
2 guns

A few minutes after the encounter with the cavalry, groups of soldiers from the 11th New York and 1st Minnesota gathered behind Ricketts' and Griffin's cannon. Other New Yorkers soon arrived as well. The 38th New York lay down directly behind Griffin's three guns near the Henry House. At the same time, Griffin redeployed two guns to Ricketts' far right (see map 27). He planned to move them to a less exposed position and send an enfilading fire down through the Confederate line of artillery pieces. Unlimbering, the artillerymen readied their cannon with shell. But Griffin saw a body of infantrymen forming to his front and ordered the cannon to be loaded with canister. Major Barry, Griffin's commander, rode up and said, "Captain, don't fire there; those are your battery support."

---

* Colonel Arthur Cummings commanded the 33d Virginia; his photo is unavailable. John Casler will represent the 33d in place of Cummings.

MAP 27

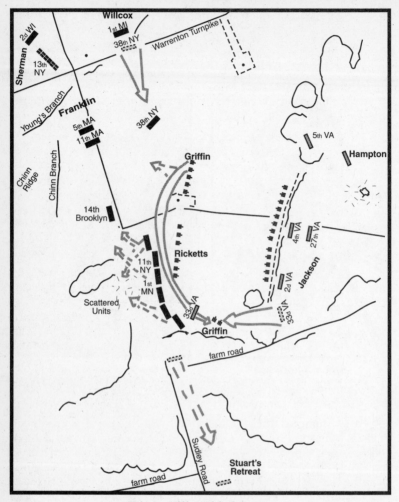

Henry Hill • Third Stage

(After the second stage the action happened so quickly no exact time can be given.) The 38th New York arrives on the hill and is ordered to lie down behind Griffin's battery. In order to send a flanking fire down the Confederate left, Griffin moves two howitzers to the far right. Meanwhile, units from the 11th New York and 1st Minnesota return to the hill. Realizing his left flank was in imminent danger of being raked by cannon fire, Confederate Colonel Cummings orders the 33d Virginia to charge Griffin's two guns. They capture the guns, and the Union infantry scatter back down the hill. Union artillerymen manning Griffin's remaining three cannon take them down the hill to safety. Ricketts' battery stays.

Griffin replied, "They are confederates; as certain as the world, they are confederates."

Barry answered, "I know they are your battery support." Obeying his commander, the Union artillerymen hesitated. The regiment, however, was the 33d Virginia.

Coming within forty yards of the cannon, they let loose a deadly volley and charged.[20] Private Casler, 33d Virginia, recalled the assault:

> *Colonel Cummings...seeing a battery of artillery taking position and unlimbering, in close proximity and in a place where it could enfilade our troops, determined to capture it before it could do any damage...Then came the command: "Attention! Forward march! Charge bayonets! Double quick!" and away we went, sweeping everything before us; but the enemy broke and fled.*[21]

Captain William Colvill, Jr., 1st Minnesota, saw the "...volley, which took effect in the centre of our regiment as well as the batteries, killing our color sergeant, and wounding three corporals of the color guard, and killing and wounding thirty men in the color company...the colors were riddled with bullets."[22]

Near the Henry House, Ricketts urged the Zouaves to help his artillerymen, but the Zouaves again "broke and ran." Griffin rode down the hill to Young's Branch and sarcastically said to Major Barry, "Major, do you think the Zouaves will support us?"

Barry replied, "I was mistaken."

Again Griffin exclaimed, "Do you think that was our support?"

The major answered, "I was mistaken."

"Yes," said Griffin, "you were mistaken all around."[23]

Union reinforcements quickly arrived and the two captured Union cannon retaken (see map 28).

(Out of ninety-five men Griffin lost twenty-seven killed, wounded, missing and fifty-five missing horses, out of 101, most of which were shot down during the battle.)

Captain William Colvill, Jr.
Company F, 1st Minnesota

MAP 28

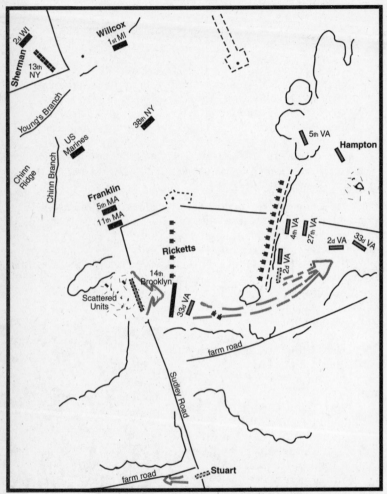

Henry Hill • Fourth and Fifth Stage

The 14th Brooklyn rushes up the hill and recaptures Griffin's two howitzers. Disorganized and outnumbered, the 33d Virginia retreats. In the confusion the 2d Virginia's left flank joins the 33d Virginia. Jackson's left flank crumbles.

FOURTH STAGE
"Red-legged Devils"

CONFEDERATE   **UNION**

Private John Casler
33d Virginia, 450

Colonel Alfred M. Wood
14th Brooklyn, 640
Wounded and captured

As the Zouaves and Minnesota soldiers again streamed down the hill, the 14th Brooklyn (nicknamed the "Red-Legged Devils" because they wore red baggy pants) ran up through their retreating ranks. Although the 33d Virginia killed many Union soldiers and captured Griffin's two howitzers, the charge badly disorganized their ranks. At only forty yards from the 33d, the Brooklyn troops unleashed a volley of fire; the 33d Virginia's ranks crumbled. Outnumbered and unsupported they fell back behind Jackson's main line. The 14th Brooklyn recaptured Griffin's guns, and continued their assault (see map 28).

FIFTH STAGE
"Few men can retire calmly under a galling fire..."

CONFEDERATE   **UNION**

Private George Baylor, age 19*
Graduate of Dickinson College, 1860.
2d Virginia, 300

Colonel Alfred M. Wood
14th Brooklyn, 640

As the 33d Virginia retreated, Colonel James Allen of the 2d Virginia, directed Companies C and G to form a new line at a right angle to the rest of the regiment. While in the process of reforming, the 14th Brooklyn fired into their left flank. Private George Baylor later recalled:

> *Companies C and G, though suffering heavily, were un-flinching and holding their own against largely superior numbers when the order was given to fall back and form a new line. This was done, no doubt, to present a front to the foe now outflanking us. It was, however, an unfortu-nate move. Few men can retire calmly under a galling fire, and the execution of this order resulted in stampeding some good soldiers...*[24]

In the confusion many of the 2d Virginians misunderstood the or-der to reform; consequently, most of the 2d joined the retiring 33d. Jackson's left was crumbling. The men of the 14th Brooklyn, nev-ertheless, continued to concentrate their fire on the deadly Con-federate artillery (see map 28). This gave Jackson time to call up his other regiments.

---

* Colonel James Allen commanded the 2d Virginia; his photo is unavailable at this time.

SIXTH STAGE
"Now d-damn you, take that."

OPPOSING COMMANDERS

CONFEDERATE   UNION

Private William Ott, age 21*
Company I, "Liberty Hall Volunteers," 4th
Virginia, 474
Former student at Washington College.
Shot through the heart, KIA.

Lieutenant Colonel E.B. Fowler
14th Brooklyn
640

Lieutenant Colonel John Echols
27th Virginia
580

* Colonel James Preston commanded the 4th Virginia, his photo is unavailable at this time.

CONFEDERATE *(cont.)*	UNION *(cont.)*

Colonel William "Extra Billy" Smith
49th Virginia Battalion
210
(Seen in a general's uniform)

Colonel Orlando B. Willcox*
1st Michigan
500
(Seen in his brigadier general's uniform)

Colonel Charles F. Fisher, age 45
6th North Carolina, 600
Shot through the head, instantly killed.

---

*Although Colonel Willcox was commander of the Second Brigade, Third Division, he led his original command, the 1st Michigan, into battle. Major A.F. Bidwell had assumed command of the 1st Michigan when Willcox was given the brigade assignment. During the battle Willcox was wounded and captured.

To meet the threat in the center, Jackson quickly rode to the 4th and 27th Virginia and shouted, "Reserve your fire until they come within 50 yards, then fire and give them the bayonet, and when you charge, yell like furies."[25] Rising, the Virginians (joined by squads of men from the 2d and 33d Virginia) let loose a blood curdling scream and, with fixed bayonets, charged. (A Confederate described the rebel yell as, "Woh-who——ey! who——ey! who——ey! Woh-who——ey! who——ey! etc." The first syllable, "woh," was short and low. "Who" was a very high and prolonged note deflecting upon "ey.")[26]

At the start, the 4th Virginia led the four-deep line.[27] The regiments, however, became intermingled. Charles R. Norris, acting captain of Company B, 27th Virginia, shouted, "Come on boys, quick, and we can whip them!!" Seconds later Norris dropped— shot through the upper left chest.[28] Private J.B. Caddall, of Company C, "Pulaski Guards," 4th Virginia, remembered:

> ...we were called to attention and ordered forward on the double-quick, and on an oblique move to the left over a stake and brush fence, through a skirt of pines and subject to a heavy fire of musketry. In a very few minutes we were in close contact with the ranks of the enemy of which a very conspicuous body was a Zouave Regiment from New York, with highly decorated uniforms, consisting of loosely fitting red breeches, blue blouses, with Turkish tassel as headgear.[29]

As the two sides collided, a vicious melée ensued. One Brooklynite jumped from behind a pine bush and lunged at Private Bronson Gwynn, 4th Virginia; the bayonet passed harmlessly through Bronson's coat between his arm and side. Gwynn pulled the bayonet from his coat and while firing his musket at the man's head stuttered, "Now d-damn you, take that," and rejoined his regiment near Ricketts' guns.[30]

Two other Confederates attacked Private Lewis Francis, 14th Brooklyn; one bayonetted him in the right knee. Private Francis later recalled the horrible incident:

> I was attacked by two rebel soldiers and wounded in the right knee with the bayonet. As I lay on the sod they kept bayoneting me until I received fourteen wounds. One then left me, the other remaining over me, when a Union soldier coming up, shot him in the breast, and he fell dead.[31]

(Amazingly, no vital organs were pierced, and he survived his wounds.)

MAP 29

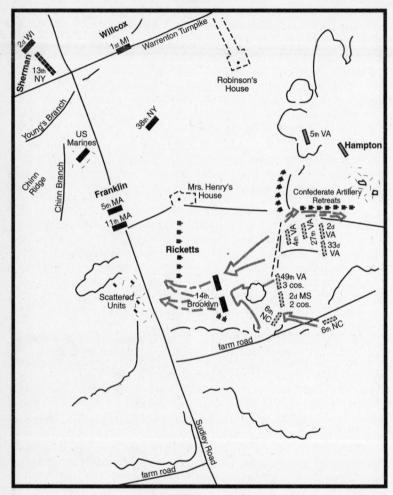

Henry Hill • Sixth Stage

Jackson orders the 4th and 27th Virginia to attack (units from the 33d and 2d Virginia also join the assault). Three companies from the 49th Virginia Battalion, two companies from 2d Mississippi and the 6th North Carolina hit the 14th Brooklyn's right flank. The New Yorkers break and fall back. Meanwhile, the Confederate cannon are ordered off the field.

The Virginia regiments suffered casualties as well. A musket ball struck Private William B. Ott, 4th Virginia, in the heart and killed him instantly; Sergeant James C. McKelsey, 33d Virginia, was killed, and Captain William Lawrence Clark, Jr., 2d Virginia, collasped near the Henry House with a thigh wound.

Near the cannon Ricketts collapsed with a thigh wound. Without infantry support the remaining Union artillerymen retreated. One lieutenant, Doug Ramsay, ran passed the "Alleghany Roughs," Company A, of the 27th Virginia. Private Clarence A. Fonerden of this company, took aim, but his comrade, Private William Fudge, fired first, killing Ramsay instantly (see map 29).[32] (In all, Ricketts' battery suffered twelve killed and fifteen wounded out of approximately ninety-four artillerymen; the majority of artillery horses lay dead behind the cannon.)

******

Private Lewis Francis, age 42
Company I, 14th Brooklyn
A drawing sixteen months after a reamputation of his right hip, succeeding amputation for a bayonet stab wound through the right knee. He received at least fourteen stab wounds. One of the wounds involved his left testis, which was removed on July 24, 1861. He returned to Brooklyn and required the constant care of a nurse. He died suddenly May 31, 1874, around the age of 55.

Sergeant James C. McKelsey
Company K, "The Shenandoah Sharpshooters," 33d Virginia
KIA

Captain William L. Clark, Jr., age 31
Company F, "Winchester Riflemen," 2d Virginia Yale University Graduate, 1849, and lawyer. Wounded around 3:00 p.m., his wound made him unfit for duty; he resigned April 14, 1862.

Lieutenant Charles Norris, age 17
Company B, 27th Virginia
Formerly a Virginia Military Institute Cadet, he was shot through the chest and killed. His coat is on display at the Manassas National Battlefield Park Visitor Center.

Lieutenant Doug Ramsay
Company I, 1st U.S. Artillery
Shot and killed while attempting to retreat. After the battle his body was stripped of all clothing except his socks.[33]

While the 4th and 27th Virginia assaulted Ricketts' battery, Colonel William Smith's Virginia battalion approached the hill. Yet, with only a small force, Smith's left flank was in danger of being turned. Fortunately for Smith, Colonel Charles Fisher's 6th North Carolina appeared on his left, hit the 14th Brooklyn's right flank and recaptured Griffin's two howitzers. The 14th's colonel, A.M. Wood, collapsed with a severe wound, and his men carried him to an ambulance; Private Augustus Brown fell dead, as did their color-bearer. Lieutenant Colonel E.B. Fowler assumed command of the regiment.

As the New Yorkers retreated they, and the newly arriving 1st Michigan, fired into the 6th North Carolina. In an attempt to rally his men, Colonel Fisher waved his sword, but a bullet struck him in the head, killing him instantly. The North Carolinians withdrew, yet Captain Isaac Avery quickly ordered a second charge; however, due to the confusion, only seven companies actively took part. The 6th again retook Griffin's guns and continued toward Ricketts' battery; but the Union troops, who had scattered into the woods west of Sudley Road, fired into the 6th's left flank, and another group of soldiers fired into their rear. Avery was slightly wounded in the leg, and Lieutenant Willie P. Mangum toppled wounded in the side. Under this galling fire, and with their colonel dead, they fell back behind Jackson's brigade (see map 30). (The 6th North Carolina lost twenty-three killed and fifty wounded.)[34] There is some debate

Private Augustus
Brown, age 22
Company C, 14th Brooklyn;
KIA

Captain Isaac Avery,
age 33
Company E, 6th North
Carolina
*(Seen in his colonel's
uniform)*

Lieutenant Willie
Preston Mangum, age
23
Company B, 6th North
Carolina
A musket ball struck him under his left arm. His Bible, which was in his left coat pocket, diverted the ball from his heart. He was, however, still severely wounded and died July 29, 1861.

among the 6th North Carolina concerning who fired upon their
rear ranks. Some speculate it was the 4th Alabama. Major Isaac
Avery theorized it was the 11th Massachusetts, wearing gray uniforms, and mistakenly identified as Confederate troops.

MAP 30

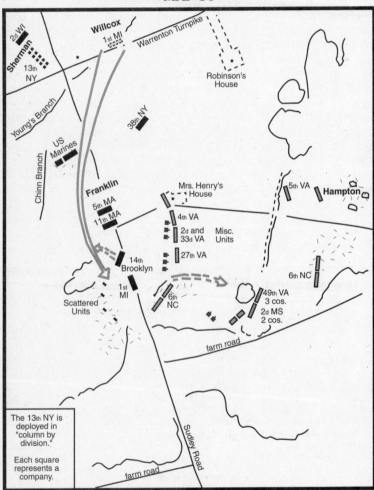

Henry Hill • Sixth Stage, *continued*

The 6th North Carolina recaptures Griffin's howitzers, but the 1st Michigan
fires into their left flank. At the same time a group of unknown soldiers fires
into the 6th's rear; they are forced to retreat.

SEVENTH STAGE
Bayonets crossed...

OPPOSING COMMANDERS

CONFEDERATE   **UNION**

Lieutenant Colonel J. Echols
27th Virginia
580

Colonel O.B. Willcox
1st Michigan
500

   After firing into the 6th North Carolina, half of the 1st Michigan charged into the Confederate line. The men crossed bayonets
and swung clubbed muskets. Private Billy Cunningham, the color-
bearer for the 1st Michigan, was shot and killed, and Private James
Glenn of the 27th Virginia captured the 1st Michigan's flag. For the
moment the Michigan soldiers had had enough, and they fell back
to Sudley Road (see map 31).[35]

MAP 31

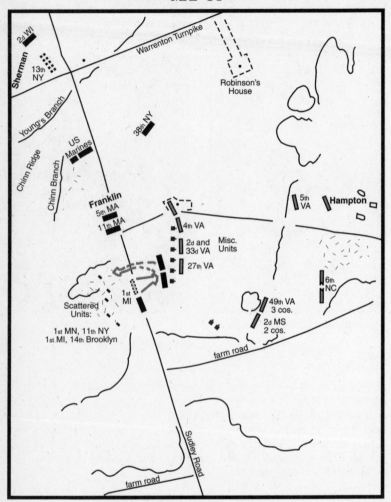

Henry Hill • Seventh Stage

Due to confusion only half of the 1st Michigan charges up the hill. The 27th
Virginia repulses their attack.

EIGHTH STAGE
"...a clear case...of self-imposed butchery."

As the Michigan troops reorganized in the road, other soldiers from the 11th New York and 14th Brooklyn joined the 1st Michigan. Minutes later the make-shift battalion headed back up the hill. Private Fonerden, 27th Virginia, recalled:

> ...only a few moments later, what may be termed the slaughter of a regiment, or battalion of red-breeched Zouaves from Brooklyn, New York, immediately in front of the 27th Regiment, was a clear case, on their part, of self-imposed butchery. They had charged us to most uncomfortable nearness, pouring upon us their deadly fire, while their own loss was so great in actual dead it has often been said, one could walk on their dead bodies over a space of several acres without touching a foot upon the ground. That sight indeed was a dreadful one, and rendered ten-fold more conspicuous by the glittering of their bright red uniforms in the gleaming sun of that hot July.[36]

Cut down by the musket fire, the Union make-shift battalion scattered down the hill, across the road and into the woods to the southwest (see map 32).

MAP 32

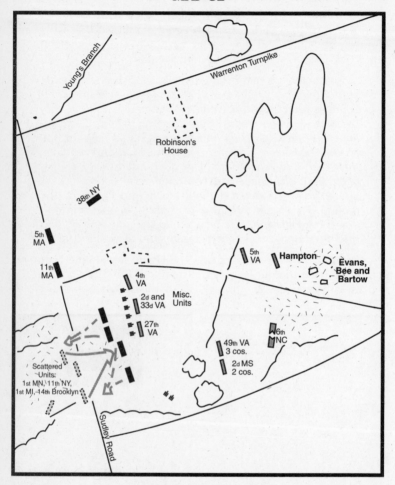

Henry Hill • Eighth Stage

Units from several Union regiments attempt to recapture Ricketts' battery. Again, they are driven back.

NINTH STAGE
"The ghastly faces of the dead..."

OPPOSING COMMANDERS

CONFEDERATE

UNION

Private James W. Crowell,
age 30*
Company C, "Pulaski Guards,"
4th Virginia
474

Colonel Samuel C. Lawrence
5th Massachusetts
850
(Seen in his brigadier general's uniform)

Lieutenant Colonel John Echols
27th Virginia
580

Colonel George Clark, Jr.
11th Massachusetts
990

---

* Colonel James Preston commanded the 4th Virginia.

While remnants of the Union battalion (1st Michigan, 11th New York, 14th Brooklyn, and 1st Minnesota) mingled in the woods, two additional regiments attempted to retake the eight guns. Together the 5th and 11th Massachusetts numbered 1,840. The Massachusetts men climbed the road bank, aligned on the colors, and stormed up the hill. The Virginians fired; the 5th Massachusetts scattered; however, the 11th Massachusetts continued up the hill. Sergeant Henry N. Blake, 11th Massachusetts, recalled the ordeal:

> *...Two men placed their hands upon their ears to exclude the noise of the musketry and artillery, and rushed to the woods in the rear of the regiment...The shells struck rifles with such force, that some were twisted into the form of circles. A cannon-ball severed the arm of a sergeant, and threw it into the face of a soldier, who supposed, from the blow and the amount of blood upon his person, that he was dangerously wounded. One man stumbled over some briers while the column was ascending a hill; and a solid shot passed over him and killed his file-leader, when he fell upon the ground. The ghastly faces of the dead, and the sufferings of the wounded, who were begging for water, or imploring aid to be carried to the hospital, moved the hearts of men who had not by long experience become callous to the sight of human agony.*[37]

On the Confederate side, Private James W. Crowell, 4th Virginia, was killed, and under the weight of the attack the 4th and 27th Virginia retreated. Captain Thompson McAllister, commander of the "Alleghany Roughs," 27th Virginia, ordered the "men to fall back and rally...Every other man except the wounded and their attendants, rallied immediately some one hundred and fifty yards in the rear..."[38]

Sergeant Henry N. Blake, age 22
Company K, 11th Massachusetts

Captain Thompson McAllister, age 50
Company A, "Alleghany Roughs," 27th Virginia

The 11th Massachusetts recaptured the eight prized cannon.
Now they stood, dressed in gray, at the top of the hill near the guns
(see map 33).

MAP 33

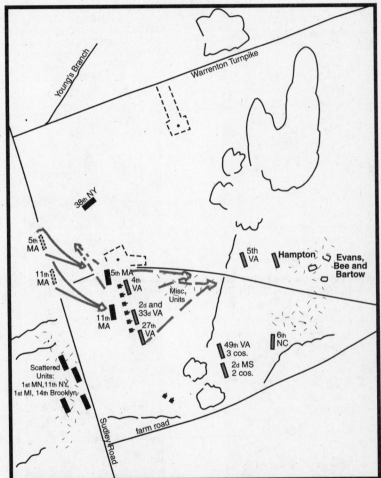

Henry Hill • Ninth Stage

**The 5th and 11th Massachusetts assault Henry Hill; immediately, the 5th breaks
and retreats. The 11th Massachusetts, however, recaptures the cannon and for a
second time Ricketts' battery is in Union hands. Dressed in their gray uniforms,
the 11th Massachusetts awaits another Confederate counterattack.**

TENTH STAGE
*"...Come with me and go yonder where
Jackson stands like a stone wall."*

OPPOSING COMMANDERS

CONFEDERATE   **UNION**

Colonel Wade Hampton
Hampton's Legion
600

Colonel George Clark, Jr.
11th Massachusetts
990

Private John Opie*
5th Virginia
380

Captain J.B. Ricketts
Company I, 1st U.S. Artillery

---

* Colonel Kenton Harper led the 5th Virginia during the battle.

With his center threatened, Beauregard rushed to the 5th Virginia and Hampton's Legion shouting, "Give them the bayonet."[39] The officers of the 5th cried out, "Close up, men!" "Steady there!" "Close up!"..."Forward!"[40]

Near Ricketts' cannon, the center of the 11th Massachusetts broke twice but reformed and held their position. Their right, however, was outflanked and forced to retreat. At the same time, Union troops to their rear, seeing the gray uniforms of the 11th, fired into their backs. Hit from the front, right, and rear the remaining soldiers of the 11th Massachusetts retreated.[41]

Black smoke covered the entire field; horses, men (dead and wounded), blanketed the ground. It was a chaotic scene. A bullet pierced Private William Woodward, 5th Virginia, and he fell near the Henry House. Woodward's friend, Private John Opie, saw another Confederate boy from Bee's brigade get hit in the forehead and fall without a groan. Opie reminisced:

> He did not tell us his name, but simply asked if he could fall in with our company. Poor boy, he died among strangers like a hero. I felt like taking him in my arms, but that was no time for sentiment; besides, it was to be expected. [Another] fellow fell, shot on the eyebrow by a spent ball, making a slight wound, and, kicking and tossing his arms about him, yelled, "O Lordy! I am killed! I am killed! O Lordy, I am dead!" I saw the fellow was not hurt much, only alarmed, and I said, "Poss," (as we called him,) "are you really killed?" "Yes, O Lordy, I am killed!" "Well," I said, "if you are really killed, why in the devil don't you stop hallooing?" He is alive to-day, but he never forgave me.[42]

As the 5th Virginia ran into the midst of Ricketts' battery, their lieutenant colonel, William H. Harman, noticed the wounded Ricketts and said, "Why, Ricketts is this you?"

Captain Ricketts replied, "Yes, but I do not know you, sir."

"We were in the Mexican War together; Harman is my name." The captain then recognized the lieutenant colonel, and the two officers shook hands.

Not all the Confederates greeted Ricketts as cordially as Lieutenant Colonel Harman. So Ricketts would not be in the line of fire the Confederates removed him from the battlefield and placed him behind their lines. As he lay helpless a group of soldiers walked by and yelled, "Knock out his brains, the d——d Yankee." No one did harm Ricketts any further, but they did shake his nerves. After the battle the Confederates took him to Richmond. While Ricketts was a prisoner Colonel Wade Hampton visited him and treated him very well. He was released five months later, in December, and returned to the Union army.[43]

While the fighting raged near Mrs. Henry's House, Bee rushed to a Confederate unit behind the Robinson House and asked, "What regiment is this?"

A captain of the 4th Alabama replied, "Why, General, don't you know your own men?" "This is what is left of the 4th Alabama."

Surprised, Bee answered, "This is all of my brigade that I can find. Will you follow me back to where the fighting is going on?" The 4th complied and, pointing to his left, Bee shouted, "Come with me and go yonder where Jackson stands like a stone wall."[44] In the confusion the regiment became separated and only about twenty Alabamians followed their general. Orderly Sergeant William O. Hudson, 4th Alabama, heard Bee exclaim, "I am a dead man, I am shot." He reeled from his saddle; Hudson and his nephew, Private J.W. Hudson, caught Bee and placed him on the ground. With the help of their comrades they took the general to the pine and oak thicket. W.O. Hudson stripped down Bee's pants and found the

Old Mexican War comrades meet on the field of battle; Lieutenant Colonel Harman and Ricketts shake hands.

Private William Woodward, age 30
5th Virginia
The night before the battle he stated to John Opie, "Boys, to-morrow I will be killed; but Opie you will survive the war!" Opie replied, "If you feel in this way, do not go into the battle." Woodward then said, "Yes, I will; I do not fear death. It is my destiny, and I will meet it like a man."[45]

bullet had passed through his abdomen. Hudson told him he "...feared his wound was mortal; but that he might live some days." The Alabama men then took him to a cabin at Manassas Junction; he died early the next morning, around 4 o'clock, while Captain John Imboden sat by his side holding his hand.[46]

At nearly the same time Bee fell, Colonel Francis Bartow suffered a mortal wound. While searching for reinforcements his horse had been shot from under him. Now, on foot, he led the 7th Georgia

Colonel Lucius J. Gartrell, age 40
Attended University of Georgia and Randolph-Macon. He was a U.S. Congressman; however, he supported states rights, and resigned from Congress when Georgia seceded. He led the 7th Georgia during the battle. He suffered a slight wound.

Captain John Imboden, age 38
Held Bee's hand at his death bed.

Brigadier General Barnard Bee, age 37
Shot through the lower abdomen; died 4:00 a.m. July 22.

Colonel Francis Bartow, age 44
Struck just above his heart; he died shortly after being wounded.

in the charge; the enemy fired, killing the 7th's color-bearer. Bartow picked up the flag and shouted, "On, my boys—we will die rather than yield or retreat." At that moment a ball struck him in the left breast just above the heart. Fellow Georgians carried Bartow from the field and placed him on the ground. He then said, "They have killed me, my brave boys, but never give up the ship—we'll whip them yet," and then he died.[47] The 7th's colonel, Lucius Gartrell, went down as well. Lucius survived his wound but his sixteen-year-old son, Henry, was killed.

Although their officers fell at a frightful rate, the Alabamians, Mississippians, Georgians, Louisianans, and the 4th South Carolina continued to fight in the woods. On the Union side, men from the 1st Michigan, 1st Minnesota, 11th New York, and 14th Brooklyn fought the make-shift Confederate battalion (see map 34).

MAP 34

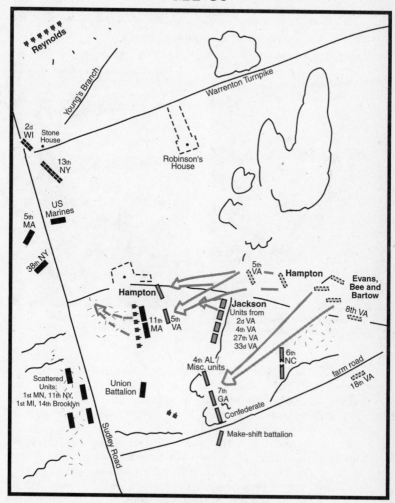

Henry Hill • Tenth Stage

Jackson orders the 5th Virginia and Hampton's Legion to retake Ricketts' battery. Other units from Jackson's brigade join in the assault. Fired upon from the front and rear, the 11th Massachusetts retreats. To their right, a Union battalion battles troops from Bee's and Bartow's brigades.

ELEVENTH STAGE
"Stop firing."

OPPOSING COMMANDERS

CONFEDERATE   **UNION**

Colonel Wade Hampton
Hampton's Legion
600

Colonel Isaac F. Quinby
13th New York
650

Ricketts' battery once again changed hands. Hiding behind the house, outhouse, sheds, bushes, caissons and cannon, the Virginians and South Carolinians awaited another Union assault. Within minutes Hampton's troops saw a regiment approaching their right flank.

The tenth Union regiment to assault the hill was the 13th New York of Colonel William T. Sherman's brigade. Advancing up the left slope of the hill, the 13th came within seventy yards of the house; there, the officers ordered the men to lie down and fire. A few Union soldiers, however, mistakenly thought the South Carolina Palmetto flag was an American flag. The New Yorkers yelled, "Stop firing." Hampton's right flank, on the other hand, did not hesitate; they poured a deadly volley into the New Yorkers. For nearly half-an-hour the 13th New York, lying in the tall grass, fought the South Carolinians (see map 35).[48]

MAP 35

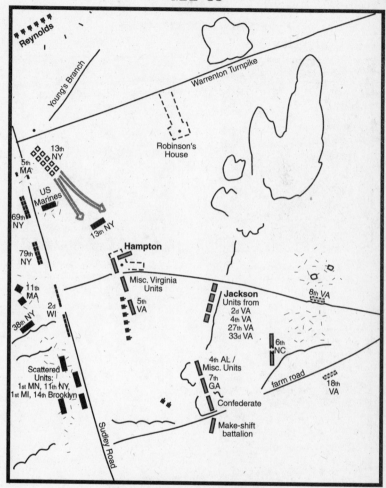

Henry Hill • Eleventh Stage

Colonel Sherman orders the 13th New York to attack. Approaching within seventy yards of the South Carolinians, the 13th hits the dirt and fights from a prone position for nearly half-an-hour.

TWELFTH STAGE
"Oh, my poor mother!"

OPPOSING COMMANDERS
CONFEDERATE   **UNION**

Colonel Wade Hampton
Hampton's Legion
600

Major James Wadsworth
Although on McDowell's staff, he
helped lead the 2d Wisconsin (900
men) into battle.
*(Seen in his brigadier general's
uniform)*

Private John Opie*
5th Virginia
380

*Colonel Kenton Harper commanded the 5th Virginia.

While the 13th New York dueled with Hampton's Legion on the Union far left, Colonel Sherman sent in his three remaining Union regiments piecemeal. The 2d Wisconsin, dressed in their militia gray, led the way.

As the Wisconsin boys waited on the Sudley Road they nervously joked and laughed. Now the time had come; with an Indian war whoop, the men jumped up and moved toward the Henry House. The Wisconsin lieutenant colonel, Harry Peck, wearing a red shirt, stood behind the right wing. Near the center, where the colors were unfurled, Major James Wadsworth, one of McDowell's staff officers, took charge. Major Duncan McDonald advanced behind the left wing.

From the start the 2d experienced trouble. In the confusion the regiment separated; the right wing, consisting of four companies, assaulted the Confederates near the woods, and the remaining six companies advanced up the hill near Ricketts' battery. On the right wing, many Wisconsin men dove behind dead horses and fired at the well-hidden Confederates. Minutes later a Wisconsin officer ran down the rear of their right flank exclaiming, "For God's sake, stop firing; you are shooting friends."[49] Many Wisconsin boys hesitated, but the Confederates again fired and the duel resumed (see map 36). A ball went through Corporal Willie Upham's neck and exited out his back bone. As he fell he cried out, "Oh, my poor Mother!"[50] (Several of his comrades helped him to a field hospital where he was captured; he survived his wound.)

Adding to the mayhem, the 79th and 69th New York, deployed on the Sudley Road, saw the Wisconsin gray uniforms and fired into their ranks. Near the house the left wing was also fired upon from three sides. The 2d rallied three times. Captain Andrew J. Langworthy, commanding Company K, later wrote about the terrible scene:

> ...all manner of projectiles known in warfare, shot, shell, grape, canister, musket and Minie balls, singing, screaming, rushing, roaring in terrible discord, and sufficient to appall a stout heart, were turned upon us. On we dashed to their breastworks, the air fairly darkened with lead and iron. Engaging them face to face, although they had every advantage of us, being covered, yet when they rose to fire the steady aims of our 2d Wisconsin made fearful havoc in their ranks, and down they tumbled by hundreds, until a pile of dead and wounded "as high as huge Olympus" lay in their trenches. But for their terror here they would have killed every one of us. It was plainly visible in their faces as they rose to fire, and we were near enough to see it.[51]

Although Langworthy exaggerated the number of dead Confederates, both ranks could plainly see the fear on the men's faces and hear the orders for their deaths. Captain John Mansfield of Company G paced along his company and shouted, "Give it to 'em, boys!" "Give it to 'em!" "Down with their accursed flag!"

MAP 36

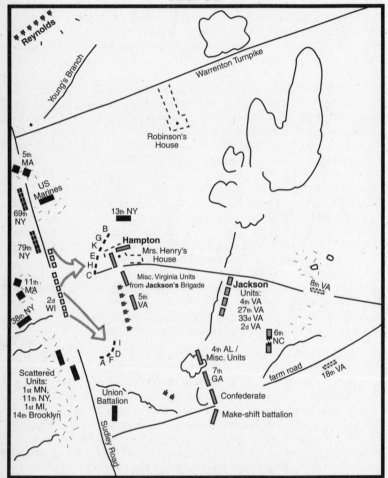

Henry Hill • Twelfth Stage

In the confusion, the 2d Wisconsin charges in two directions. The 5th Virginia, Hampton's Legion, and miscellaneous units from Jackson's other regiments, meet the attack.

On the other side, some Wisconsin boys thought they heard the Virginians yell, "Kill them!" "Mow them down, the Northern Abolition sons of bitches!" "Give them no quarter!"[52]

The 2d, however, could not withstand salvos from three sides, and after ten to fifteen minutes they retreated to Sudley Road (see map 37). (During the battle, the 2d Wisconsin lost 24 killed, 65 wounded and 23 missing.)

Afterward, dissatisfied with the leadership of their commanders during the conflict, the Wisconsin captains invited Colonel S. Park Coon, Lieutenant Colonel Peck, and Major McDonald to resign. The three willingly and quickly complied.[53]

Corporal Willie Upham, age 20
Company F, "Belle City Rifles,"
2d Wisconsin

Captain Andrew J. Langworthy
Company K, "Wisconsin Rifles,"
2d Wisconsin

Captain John Mansfield
Company G, "Portage Light Guard,"
2d Wisconsin
(Seen in a field grade uniform—
major or higher)

In the battle Peck and Major McDonald placed themselves in the rear of the 2d, as Hardee's tactics taught the regular officers. Peck's Wisconsin regiment, however, consisted of volunteers—not professionals—and, therefore, needed to be led.

MAP 37

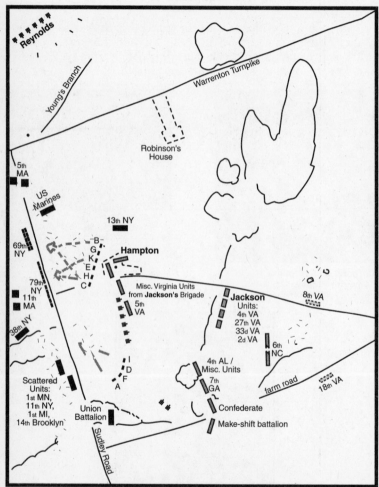

Henry Hill • Twelfth Stage, *continued*

In another case of mistaken identity, Union troops positioned behind the gray-clad 2d Wisconsin, fire into their backs. Struck from the front and rear, the 2d is compelled to retreat.

THIRTEENTH STAGE
"Come on, my brave Highlanders!"

OPPOSING COMMANDERS

CONFEDERATE   **UNION**

Colonel Wade Hampton
Hampton's Legion
600

Colonel James Cameron
79th New York Highlanders
895

Private John Opie*
5th Virginia
380

*Colonel Kenton Harper led the 5th Virginia.

As the 2d Wisconsin fell back, Sherman ordered the 79th New York into the fray. In the confusion many Wisconsin soldiers joined the New York regiment. The 79th's commander, Colonel James Cameron, placed himself to the right front and shouted, "Come on, my brave Highlanders!" One Highlander, Private William Todd, later described the attack.

> When half way up the hill, on the brow of which the enemy was posted, we received his first volley, and many of our comrades fell. This threw us into some confusion, but un-der the directions of our officers we reformed and pressed on, delivering our fire and receiving another murderous volley, in return, by which Colonel Cameron was killed [he was shot through the chest]; this, with the constant fire of shells from their batteries, somewhat staggered us, but reforming we again pressed forward...Suddenly some one cried out, "Cease firing! you're shooting your own men!" "No they ain't!" another replied; "don't you see they are firing at us?"...Contradictory orders again rang out—"Blaze away, boys! they're only trying to deceive us!" "Cease fir-ing, I tell you! They are our own men!" By this time the line on the hill-top had formed and all doubt as to their iden-tity vanished. "Ready! aim! fire!" came from that column, and a shower of bullets crashed through our already torn and bleeding ranks![54]

A Wisconsin corporal clearly remembered his experience, "I went up past the tall rebel whom I had shot through the breast about a second or so after he had hurrahed for Beauregard, and whose great blue eyes stared so wildly that I think of them often still, and presume I always shall."[55]

The 79th New York and remnants of the 2d Wisconsin wa-vered, tried to rally, but the Virginians and South Carolinians sent another lethal volley into their ranks. The men fell back to the road and sought shelter from the deadly musketry (see map 38). (Thirty-two Highlanders were killed, 51 wounded, and 115 were missing.)

On the Confederate side, Hampton's Legion and the 5th Vir-ginia beat back four Union regiments in nearly forty minutes of fighting. Hampton lay near the Henry House with slight head and ankle wounds. (The bullet grazed his left temple.)[56] Captain James Conner assumed command of the Legion. The Confederates were extremely thirsty and tired when two fresh Union regiments charged into their ranks.

MAP 38

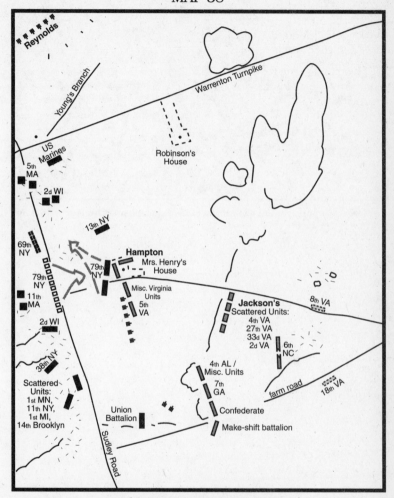

Reynolds

Young's Branch

Warrenton Turnpike

US Marines

Robinson's House

5th MA

2d WI

13th NY

Hampton

Mrs. Henry's House

69th NY

79th NY

79th NY

11th MA

Misc. Virginia Units

5th VA

Jackson's Scattered Units:
4th VA
27th VA
33d VA
2d VA

8th VA

6th NC

2d WI

38th NY

4th AL / Misc. Units

7th GA

farm road

18th VA

Scattered Units:
1st MN,
11th NY,
1st MI,
14th Brooklyn

Union Battalion

Confederate

Make-shift battalion

Sudley Road

Henry Hill • Thirteenth Stage

The 79th New York Highlanders assault Henry Hill; their colonel, James Cameron, is killed. With the death of their colonel, the Highlanders retreat.

A nineteenth-century artist's rendition of the Highlanders at Bull Run and Colonel Cameron's death.

FOURTEENTH STAGE
"Come on, boys! you have got your chance at last."

OPPOSING COMMANDERS

CONFEDERATE   **UNION**

Captain James Conner
Hampton's Legion
600
(Seen in his general's uniform)

Colonel Michael Corcoran
69th New York "Irish" Regiment
998

Private John Opie
5th Virginia
380

Colonel Hobart J. Ward
38th New York, "Second Scott Life
Guard"
665

Sherman's last unscathed regiment was the 69th New York. Stripped of their knapsacks and overcoats, the Irishmen, joined by the 38th New York, rushed up the hill. Captain Thomas Meagher rode at the head of the 69th shouting, "Come on, boys! you have got your chance at last."[57] His company, a special Zouave detachment, along with the other Irishmen, surged forward.

Confederate Lieutenant Richard Lewis, a member of a 4th South Carolina company which had become intermingled with Hampton's Legion, recalled:

> *Our company was lying behind the plank and rail fence in front of the Henry house at one time in the fight, and the enemy commenced shelling us furiously, and the Yankee Zouaves, who were dressed in red, commenced charging us and they scared us pretty badly. We started to run, but Captain Kilpatrick drew his sword and ordered us to lie down, and said if any of us ran he would hew us down; but Johnson Wright, his negro, who had been with us fighting up to that time, was lying behind the rail fence, when a shell struck the fence and knocked a rail off on him. Kilpatrick's sword never reached him, for he says he never stopped long enough to get his breath between there and Manassas Junction.[58]*

The South Carolinians held their position momentarily, but under the combined weight of the infantry and artillery they finally retreated to the pine trees.

On the Union right, Colonel Hobart Ward, 38th New York, quickly detailed several of his men to pull three cannon off the hill. The New Yorkers managed to drag the guns back three-hundred yards to Sudley Road. Meanwhile, Ward saw to the right the makeshift Union battalion scatter from the woods. At double-quick the 38th rushed into the woods. Joined by fragments of the 1st Michigan, 1st Minnesota, 14th Brooklyn, and 11th New York, the Union battalion engaged in a "sharp and spirited" skirmish (see map 39).[59] Outnumbered, the Confederates fell back, and once again Henry Hill was recaptured. To many Union troops it seemed the field had been won. The Confederate commanders, however, refused to call a general retreat. Instead, they pushed forward two fresh regiments.

MAP 39

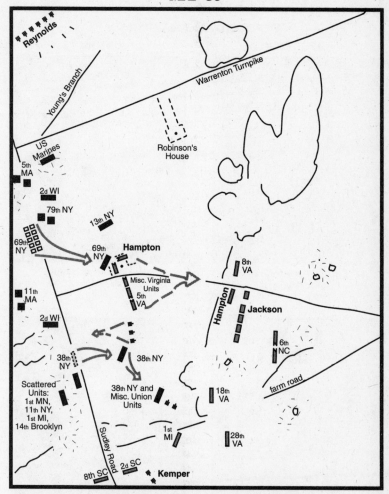

Henry Hill • Fourteenth Stage

The 69th New York "Irish" Regiment breaks through the Confederate line. On the 69th's right flank, the 38th New York, 1st Michigan, and miscellaneous Union units, battle in the woods.

FIFTEENTH STAGE
"...remember Ireland and Fontenoy."

OPPOSING COMMANDERS

CONFEDERATE   **UNION**

Colonel Eppa Hunton
8th Virginia
(Seen in a general's uniform)

Colonel Isaac F. Quinby
13th New York
650

Captain James Conner
Hampton's Legion
600*

Colonel Michael Corcoran
69th New York
988

*Hampton's Legion had been fighting since 11:30 a.m, and they had been suffering casualties almost the entire time. It was now about 3:45–4:00 p.m.

CONFEDERATE *(cont.)*

Colonel Joseph B. Kershaw, age 39*
2d South Carolina
(Seen here in his brigadier general's uniform)

UNION *(cont.)*

Colonel Hobart J. Ward
38th New York
665

Captain Thomas Meagher, age 37
Company K, 69th New York

---

*Colonel Robert E. Withers, commander of the 18th Virginia, also led his regiment into the battle at this time. A painting of him can be found in the Virginia Historical Society's collection.

While Ward's regiment skirmished in the woods, the 69th continued up the slope of Henry Hill. Using the pine trees as cover, the Confederates showered the Irishmen with lead. The Irish Brigade historian recounted:

> After each repulse, the regiment formed and charged right up on the batteries, Meagher's company of Zouaves suffered desperately, their red dress making them a conspicuous mark for the enemy. When Meagher's horse was torn from under him by a rifled cannon ball, he jumped up, waved his sword, and exclaimed, "Boys! look at that flag— remember Ireland and Fontenoy."...Colonel Corcoran rallied and charged with them in every assault.[60]

To counter this attack, Captain Conner redeployed Hampton's Legion to the right of Colonel Robert E. Withers' 18th Virginia. Withers rode to a group of officers situated behind his regiment; there he asked Beauregard for orders. The general stated, "Change your direction to the left oblique and charge across the Sudley Road."[61] Confronted by the combined force of the 8th and 2d South Carolina, 18th Virginia, Hampton's Legion, and the 8th Virginia, the thirteen Union regiments—disorganized and scattered from the Henry House to Sudley Ford—began leaving the field (see map 40). The Confederates, after approximately two hours, regained control of the hill and eight of the prized Union cannon. The battle, however, was not yet over.

Casualties on Henry Hill

Nearly 193 Confederates were killed and another 326 wounded. The Union suffered 285 killed and 647 wounded—in all, 1,452 Americans lay in and around the plateau, Mrs. Henry included.* (Approximately 104 artillery horses from Griffin's and Ricketts' battery were also killed or wounded.)

---

*The 33d Virginia suffered 146 killed and wounded out of 400, the heaviest Confederate casualties during the Henry Hill fighting. Colonel Gorman's 1st Minnesota sustained the highest Union casualties. Out of 900, 150 were either killed or wounded.

MAP 40

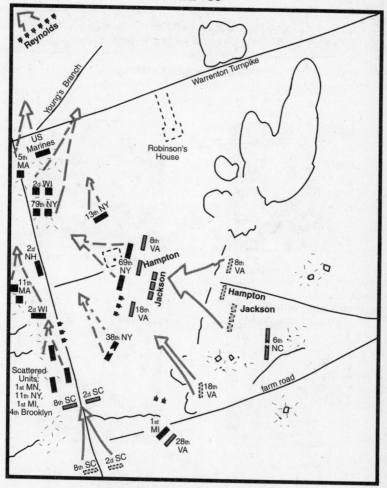

Henry Hill • Fifteenth Stage

Confederate reinforcements arrive and push the Union regiments off Henry Hill.
The Union troops around the hill begin a general retreat.

Chapter 10

CHINN FARM

FIRST STAGE
"The Vermont Second...deliberately fired with rapidity."

OPPOSING COMMANDERS

| CONFEDERATE | UNION |

CONFEDERATE   UNION

Brigade Commander: **Brigade Commander:**

**Brigadier General
Milledge L. Bonham
1,200***

**Colonel Oliver O. Howard
4,030†**

Regiment Commanders: **Regiment Commanders:**

**Colonel Joseph B. Kershaw
2d South Carolina**

**Colonel Hiram G. Berry
4th Maine
*(Seen in his brigadier
general's uniform)***

---

*Bonham's entire brigade numbered 4,961. During the conflict, however, only two of his six infantry regiments participated (the 2d and 8th South Carolina).

†This number indicates how many men were mustered into the brigade. Because of the intense heat and marching about half the men dropped out and did not actually participate in the battle.

150

CONFEDERATE *(cont.)*

Regimental Commanders:

UNION *(cont.)*

Regimental Commanders:

Colonel Ellerbe Boggan Crawford Cash
8th South Carolina
(Postwar)

Colonel Henry Whiting
2d Vermont

Brigade Commander:

Colonel Arnold Elzey
1,700*

*About 2,900 Confederates attacked Howard's 2,000 troops on the Chinn farm.

As Brigadier General Milledge Bonham's and Colonel Arnold Elzey's brigades extended the Confederate left flank (about 3:30 p.m.), McDowell ordered Union Colonel Oliver Howard to bring up his brigade.[1]

Howard, however, was a mile away, and his men had to sprint in the hot, humid July weather. Many soldiers dropped out of the ranks, exhausted and suffering from heat stroke. Consequently, his brigade arrived on Mr. Benjamin Chinn's farm* with only half its strength. Around 4:00 p.m. Howard's first regiments, the 2d Vermont and 4th Maine, deployed on the ridge. In his after-action report Colonel Henry Whiting of the 2d Vermont wrote:

> [A] line was formed; we marched up the hill-side, and about half the distance to the next eminence, about two hundred yards in front, where the infantry and artillery of the rebels were stationed in force. The Vermont Second formed in line, and deliberately fired with rapidity from fifteen to twenty rounds.[2]

Whiting then ordered his regiment forward. Yet, only the right company heard his directive. Marching a short distance, the Union company discovered a battery of Confederate cannon to their right. Without the support of the entire regiment they retreated, and the remaining nine companies followed (see map 41). Colonel Howard quickly sent in his remaining units, the 3d and 5th Maine.

Just as the 3d and 5th Maine formed near the Chinn farm, the Confederate brigades fired into their front and right flank. The Maine men vollied back; however, the Union troops could not see Elzey's Confederate brigade, which was concealed in the woods. Private George W. Bicknell, 5th Maine, recalled the frustrating situation:

> ...Fire at what? About five hundred yards in our front was a belt of woods, though not a Johnny in sight. Into this wood we poured our volleys, though wholly ignorant whether our efforts were of any use or not; but still we worked with a will...But what is that? Clear rings the words, "cease firing," "about face," "in retreat march..."[3]

---

*On the modern maps this area is referred to as Chinn Ridge; "Chinn Ridge" is a park service applied place name. The historically correct name for this area is the Chinn farm because there are no historic documents which refer to it as "Chinn Ridge."[4] At the time of the Civil War Mr. Benjamin Chinn owned a farm in this area, and they named their house "Hazel Plain."

MAP 41

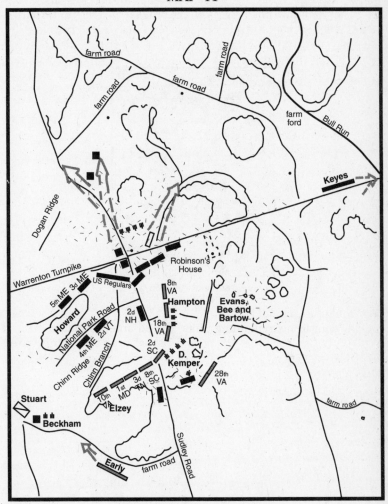

Chinn Ridge • First Stage

Union Colonel Howard deploys the 4th Maine and 2d Vermont on the Chinn
farm. The right company of the 2d Vermont advances but is hit by Confederate
cannon fire. Without the support of the entire regiment the company retires and
the rest of the 2d Vermont follows.

In the confusion, Bicknell and his comrades misheard the command. Only the right wing of the 5th Maine had been ordered to fall back, not the entire regiment. With the 5th Maine in retreat Howard's remaining regiments broke and started back to Centreville, Virginia (see map 42).

Private George W. Bicknell, age 24
5th Maine
(Seen here in his lieutenant's uniform)

MAP 42

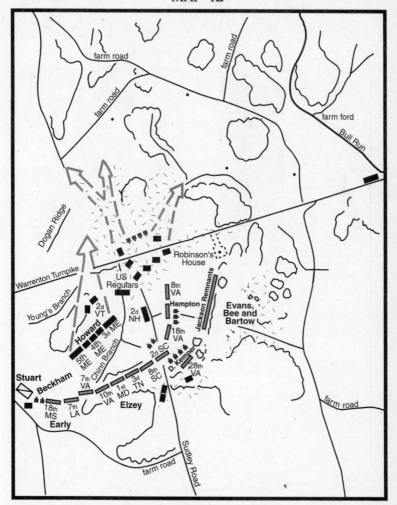

Chinn Ridge • Second Stage

As the 2d Vermont falls back, Howard deploys his remaining two regiments (5th and 3d Maine). His brigade is sorely outnumbered and outflanked by Confederate reinforcements. Consequently, Howard's men are compelled to withdraw. McDowell's army is now in full retreat.

CHINN FARM/YOUNG BRANCH
SECOND STAGE
"...we were being surrounded."

UNION COMMANDERS

Major George Sykes
U.S. Regular Infantry battalion
*(Seen here in his major general's
uniform)*

**Lieutenant Colonel
Francis Fiske**
2d New Hampshire

To cover the withdrawal of the Union army Major George Sykes' U.S. Regular Infantry battalion and the 2d New Hampshire deployed on Mr. Chinn's farm and Sudley Road. It was a tense moment compounded by a Confederate cavalry charge. First Lieutenant Eugene Carter wrote:

> *We found that our troops were all leaving the field, and that we were being surrounded. One or two squadrons of cavalry were trying to get on our flank, but we formed a square so quickly that they became convinced who we were, and kept out of range of our rifles.*[5]

While the cavalrymen kept a fair distance from the Regulars, the Confederate artillerymen and infantrymen fired into their ranks. Outnumbered, the 2d New Hampshire and the Regulars faced by the rear rank and quickly walked off the field (see map 43).[6]

MAP 43

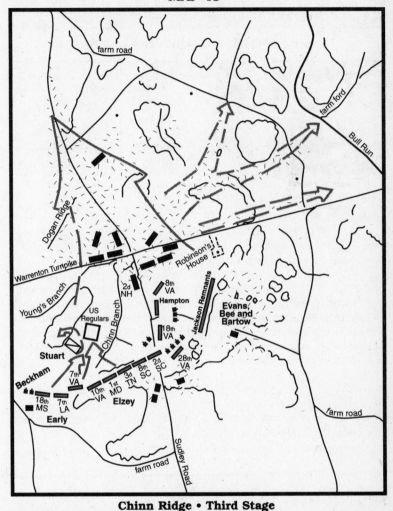

Chinn Ridge • Third Stage

The U.S. Regulars and 2d New Hampshire cover the Union retreat. Jeb Stuart's cavalry charges the U.S. Regulars on the Chinn farm, but the cavalry are repulsed. Nevertheless, the Union units, sorely outnumbered, must fall back.

CHINN FARM
THIRD STAGE
"Stars and Stripes! Give it to them, boys!"

CONFEDERATE BRIGADE COMMANDERS

**Brigadier General
Milledge L. Bonham
1,200**

**Colonel Arnold Elzey
1,700**

**Colonel Jubal Early
1,400**

Having fired upon the Union line, Confederate Colonel Arnold Elzey looked through his field glasses (binoculars) and studied the battle line in front of him. He then dropped his hand and, with eyes lighted, yelled, "Stars and Stripes! Stars and Stripes! Give it to them, boys!"[7] Orderly Sergeant McHenry Howard, 1st Maryland, remembered they fired twice and then, with a hoarse cry, charged with fixed bayonets. Joined by Early's brigade, the men looked more like a mob, every soldier racing to be the first in line. While passing a pasture they discovered an abundant crop of blackberries. Having not eaten in nearly thirty-six hours, thirsty and undisciplined, they stopped to eat the fruit. The officers ran to the men and began swearing at them in an attempt to rally them around the colors. Reluctantly, the men complied and resumed the charge. When they finally reached the top of the ridge, the Union troops were gone (see map 43). After approximately ten and one-half hours of fighting, 6:00 a.m.–4:30 p.m., the first battle of the Civil War was over.

**Orderly Sergeant
McHenry Howard, age 22
Maryland Guard, 1st
Maryland, CSA**

Chapter 11

THE RETREAT

Thousands of Union men streamed toward Bull Run. Burnside's, Porter's, Howard's, Willcox's, and Franklin's brigades recrossed at Sudley Ford. Many units were completely disorganized and some frightened individuals ran frantically. Private Bicknell, 5th Maine, candidly stated, "How we traveled! Nobody tired now. Every one for himself, and having a due regard for individuality, each gave a special attention to the rapid momentum of his legs."[2]

Sergeant Merritt, 1st Minnesota, retreated with two of his comrades. Yet Merritt's wounded leg prevented him from walking; therefore, he paid to ride a teamster's horse. In order not to jam his injured leg between two of the horses, which were still hitched to a wagon, he rode backwards. Merritt was a sad sight to behold: his hair stuck straight up, matted with leaves and grass, his face covered with blood and dirt, a horrible bloody leg wound, riding a horse backwards while holding onto its tail. He rode like this for about four miles until he reached Centreville.[3] Another band of Minnesotans appropriated whiskey from an ambulance kit which "knocked 'em all silly."[4]

Near the farm ford, Sherman's and Keyes' brigades double-backed across Bull Run (see map 44). Like the other units, their regiments intermingled. Some men ran; others, exhausted, slowly walked up the Warrenton Pike, as artillery shells exploded in and around them, and Confederate cavalry constantly harassed them.

The Confederate artillery especially aimed for the Cub Run bridge where wagons, soldiers, and civilians desperately crowded and made easy targets. Shells dropped so frequently that the soldiers crawled across the bridge on their hands and knees; it was a very trying time. Private Elisha H. Rhodes saw his captain, S. James Smith, 2d Rhode Island, cut in two by a round shot. Rhodes escaped injury and his regiment arrived in Washington around 12 o'clock noon, July 22.[5]

MAP 44

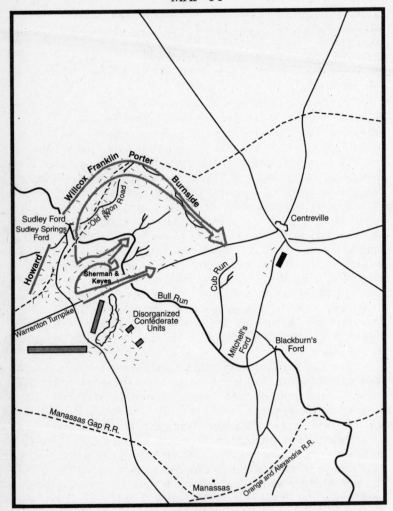

Willcox Franklin Porter

Burnside

Old Wagon Road

Sudley Ford
Sudley Springs
Ford

Centreville

Howard

Sherman &
Keyes

Bull Run

Cub Run

Disorganized
Confederate
Units

Warrenton Turnpike

Mitchell's
Ford

Blackburn's
Ford

Manassas Gap R.R.

Orange and Alexandria R.R.

Manassas

Union Retreat

**Disorganized, McDowell's army recrosses Bull Run: some soldiers slowly walk-
ing, others running for a few miles. No Union soldiers ran twenty-six miles back
to Washington; many men collapsed in Centreville and completed the march
several hours later.**

Union artillerymen also had an arduous time. On the east side of Stone Bridge Lieutenant Peter Hains, with his thirty-pounder, had been frustratingly inactive all day. Late in the afternoon McDowell saw Hains and asked, "What are you doing there with that gun?"

The lieutenant answered, "Awaiting orders, sir."

"Get it out, get it out quick," McDowell exclaimed and rode off.[6]

McDowell reached Centreville about 5:45 p.m. and directed Colonel Dixon S. Miles to hold the town until the Union men had passed through. McDowell then rode to Fairfax Court House and wrote to one of his staff officers:

> *The men having thrown away their haversacks in the battle and left them behind, are without food; have eaten nothing since breakfast. We are without artillery ammunition. The larger part of the men are a confused mob, entirely demoralized. It was the opinion of all the commanders that no stand could be made this side of the Potomac. We will, however, make the attempt at Fairfax Court-House.[7]*

While McDowell sent out directives, Hains, with only ten horses and eleven men, began the arduous task of pulling their six-thousand-pound gun down the Warrenton Pike. The Union artillerymen stopped to rest at the Spindle house, where hundreds of stragglers and wounded crowded around a well. Hains, sick with dysentery and a headache, drank nearly a bucketful of water. Having refreshed himself, he looked up to see cavalry forming in a field across the road. Hains quickly shouted to the Union stragglers, "Fall in here! Fall in, men! Rally about me, quick—that's rebel cavalry!" Only three men came to his side. Hains furiously yelled, "Fire, for God's sake, fire—that's Virginia cavalry!" The infantrymen disagreed and insisted the horsemen were Union cavalry. Artilleryman Lieutenant Edmund Kirby, however, realized the imminent danger. He unlimbered two cannon and ordered his men to load double charges of canister. The gunners fired, but the horsemen continued their charge. Hains fired his pistol and shouted, "Fire, fire, you infernal fools, fire!" The cannoneers reloaded and showered the Virginia horsemen with canister.

> *...The horses reared upward and fell over upon their riders; some, frantic under awful wounds, dashed into their own ranks and rolled the line up. Men toppled out of their saddles, and their horses ran madly for shelter...The black-bearded leader yelled furiously for them to charge the guns...[8]*

Confederate Colonel Richard C.W. Radford's battalion of cavalrymen came within thirty yards. At last, the Union infantrymen fired. Disorganized and bloodied the horsemen fell back to regroup. Hains ran after them and emptied his six-shooter. Out of ammunition, Lieutenant Hains discontinued his pursuit, and because he needed a weapon, he took a dead Virginia cavalryman's sword.

Meanwhile, Kirby limbered up his cannon and started back up the pike. Hains as well rejoined his "plodding" gun. Minutes later Lieutenant Colonel Thomas Munford's Confederate cavalry battalion attacked another Union battery. This time the artillerymen had no time to fire, and the battery was captured. It was nearly nightfall. Tired, hungry, and thirsty Hains ordered his men to unhitch the horses and abandon their beloved cannon. Before leaving, however, he jammed a priming iron into the vent, rendering the cannon useless, and headed toward Centreville.[9]

As the Union stragglers arrived in Centreville, the 1st and 2d New Jersey regiments attempted to organize the fugitives. They appealed to their patriotism, honor, and sense of duty, but the soldiers did not fall into ranks. Finally, the New Jersey regiments charged bayonets; officers drew their swords and pistols and threatened the disorderly mob. Being persuaded, many of the soldiers fell in line with the New Jersey regiments. To cover their retreat Lieutenant Colonel Robert McAllister's 1st New Jersey acted as rear-guard.[10]

Sunday, July 21, was one of the longest days in their short military careers. The Union men had awakened at 2:00 a.m., marched six to twelve miles, fought for nearly ten and one-half hours and walked back to Centreville. From there, with only a few hours rest, or none at all, the soldiers resumed their retreat to Washington, D.C. In all, they had walked about forty-five miles within thirty-six hours, sustained merely on crackers, water, and coffee (or liquor).[11] By Monday most had reached the capital. The army, however, was badly demoralized and disorganized.

A few days later a civilian recognized a Fire Zouave (11th New York) near Washington market and asked, "What the devil are you doing here, got leave of absence?" The New Yorker exclaimed, "No, I got the word to 'fall back' at Bull Run, and nobody has told me to halt, so I have kept on retreatin' ever since, and got away here."[12] Within the next several weeks this undisciplined and frivolous attitude would change.

Captain S. James Smith
Company I, 2d Rhode
Island
While he was attempting to
cross the Cub Run bridge a
round shot cut him in two.

Lieutenant Peter Hains
Seen with captured sword.

**Lieutenant Edmund
Kirby**
Company I, 1st U.S.
Artillery
(Ricketts' battery)

VIGNETTE:
BROTHER AGAINST BROTHER: THE MCALLISTERS

During the battle for Henry Hill Captain Thompson McAllister's Company A, "Alleghany Roughs," 27th Virginia, aided in repulsing the Union regiments. As the Union soldiers walked/fled back to Centreville, they met the 1st and 2d New Jersey regiments who tried to persuade the soldiers to fall back into line and regain some organization. The majority of soldiers regrouped; the 1st New Jersey commanded by Lieutenant Colonel Robert McAllister (Thompson's brother) acted as rear-guard.

The McAllister brothers grew up in Juniata County, Pennsylvania where their father, Judge William McAllister, owned a small farm. Sarah Thompson McAllister gave birth to her second son, Thompson, on August 30, 1811; two years later, Robert was born on June 1, 1813. The brothers worked hard together in the classroom and on the farm; both also enjoyed studying military tactics and practicing drill. At an early age, Thompson organized an artillery company and held drill four times a year. In 1839, he married Lydia M. Addams and moved to Franklin County; the company then elected Robert as captain. Ten years later, 1849, Thompson moved to Covington, Virginia, situated in Alleghany County, Shenandoah Valley. There, he purchased 2,200 acres and became a leader within his community. When war appeared inevitable he organized the "Alleghany Light Infantry," nicknamed, "Alleghany Roughs" and placed them at the disposal of the governor of Virginia. On April 17, 1861, Virginia delegates voted to secede from the Union; the McAllister brothers, once best friends, found themselves enemies.

In the spring of 1861 Robert was working in Oxford, New Jersey for the Delaware, Lackawanna and Western Railroad. After Lincoln's call to arms Robert organized a company at Oxford and left for Trenton. There, Governor Charles S. Olden of New Jersey commissioned him lieutenant colonel of the 1st New Jersey.

Fortunately for the brothers the 27th Virginia and 1st New Jersey did not meet at First Manassas. After the battle, Thompson was afflicted with camp fever. Weakened by the fever and wearisome marches, Thompson reluctantly tendered his resignation. He returned to Covington, and was placed in command of the home-guard and reserves in Alleghany County until the end of the war. Robert was commissioned colonel of the 11th New Jersey on June 30, 1862; breveted brigadier general for his actions at Boydton Plank

Road, October 1864, and finally given the rank of major general for meritorious conduct throughout the war. In four years of service he participated in every battle with the Army of the Potomac (except for Second Manassas, South Mountain, and Antietam).

After the war there was a long silence between the brothers. In a letter never sent to Robert, Thompson wrote:

Sweet Chalybeate Springs, July 9, 1870.

My Very Dear Brother:

Such I have ever regarded you and until I have further knowledge, must still regard you, although the long silence would indicate anything else. The years spent in deadly combat in which you and I were actors on opposite sides explains itself, but that five years should have elapsed since the close of the war without any communication between us is astonishing indeed.

Out of this contest you came victorious; we lost everything but our land and our honor, the former of which, for a time at least, we held by an uncertain tenure, but the last was as enduring as life itself. To have opened a correspondence with you under the circumstances [the views which General McAllister held as to the South] was a compromise of honor which I did not feel at liberty to make. Now that your long-looked-for letter has come I would not have delayed answering it a single day but for physical disablility...[13]

Although Thompson did not send this letter, the brothers—including their oldest brother, Nelson—met in New York. Due to chronic fatigue, Thompson visited several physicians, and the doctors pronounced his condition incurable. (No specific disease was given.)

When the McAllister brothers parted for home all three knew it was their last meeting. On March 13, 1871, at the age of sixty, Thompson McAllister died. Robert survived his brother by twenty years; he died February 23, 1891, and was buried at Belvidere, New Jersey.[14]

Captain Thompson McAllister, age 50
Company A, "Alleghany Roughs," 27th
Virginia
(Seen in civilian attire)

Lieutenant Colonel Robert McAllister,
age 48
1st New Jersey

Chapter 12

THE PURSUIT

Having recaptured Ricketts' battery, the Confederates turned several of the cannon around and began shelling the retreating Union troops. Beauregard rode along Henry Hill shouting, "The day is ours! The day is ours!"[1] He then directed the 18th Virginia, Hampton's Legion, 2d and 8th South Carolina, and Captain Del Kemper's battery toward the Stone Bridge. About one mile south of the Cub Run bridge, Kemper unlimbered two of his cannon in the road and began bombarding the old country road and the turn-pike. A wagon overturned on the Cub Run bridge, and the entire area became a traffic jam. To make matters worse for the Union soldiers, after Kemper had shelled the area, Colonel Richard Radford's and Lieutenant Colonel Thomas T. Munford's horsemen charged into them. The Black Horse troop led the attack. With no alternative the Union troops fled for their lives, leaving their pos-sessions behind.

Later in the evening Confederate scouts reported to Beauregard that the Union army was threatening his line at Union Mills Ford. This report turned out to be false. Confederate scouts mistakenly thought Brigadier General David R. Jones' troops, who were re-turning from their expedition, were Union soldiers.

Jones, as directed by Beauregard, sent his regiments—5th South Carolina, 17th and 18th Mississippi—across McLean's Ford at approximately 2:30 p.m. While the Confederates on Henry Hill successfully checked the Union assaults, a Union brigade deployed near McLean's Ford, on the eastern slopes, repulsed Jones' regi-ments. Colonel Micah Jenkins, commander of the 5th South Caro-lina, later reported that his regiment

> ...advanced quickly over very difficult ground. While gal-lantly charging in fine order our friends in the rear poured in upon me heavy fires of musketry, cutting us up sadly. This compelled a halt, which I made upon gaining the brow of the hill upon which the enemy was stationed. Here,

Colonel Micah Jenkins, age 26
5th South Carolina
Graduate of South Carolina Military
Academy

Private Thomas W. "Bunk" Fowler,
age 27
Company E, 5th South Carolina
KIA, near McLean's Ford. He was buried at
Gilead Baptist Church, Union, South Carolina.

under a terrific fire of shell, I reformed and dressed my
lines, and reloaded such guns as had been fired. Expect-
ing the reserve to form to the rear to my support, I made
every preparation to renew my charge upon the batteries,
when I discovered that I was isolated in the presence of
the enemy's guns, cavalry, and three or four regiments of
infantry.[2]

During this attack three members of the 5th South Carolina were
killed, including Private Thomas W. "Bunk" Fowler. Outnumbered,
the 5th South Carolina and the other two Mississippi regiments
retreated back toward McLean's Ford and Union Mills Ford.

Because the Confederate scouts falsely identified Jones' brigade as Union troops Beauregard halted the pursuit, and the majority of his regiments returned to Bull Run.[3] The 8th South Carolina, however, remained near Cub Run in order to secure the captured goods (see map 45). By the time Beauregard realized his right
flank was in no danger, the sun had set, and it was too dark to
resume following McDowell's force.

During the retreat the Confederates, especially the Black Horse
Troop, seized a number of prisoners, and an abundance of military
supplies.

MAP 45

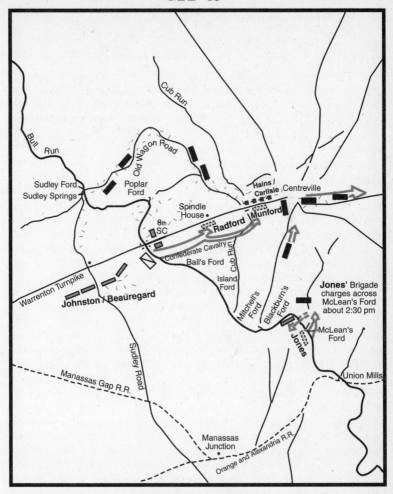

Confederate Pursuit

Confederate Colonel Radford's cavalry squadron attacks Hains and the Union troops around Mrs. Spindle's house. Hains escapes and his men drag the 6,000-pound cannon across the Cub Run bridge. Confederate Lieutenant Colonel Munford's cavalry squadron then strikes Carlisle's battery. Hains and Carlisle abandon their cannon. A shell from Confederate Captain Del Kemper's guns overturns a wagon on the Cub Run bridge and the Union troops are forced to cross Cub Run where ever possible. Beauregard stops the pursuit when he receives information that Union soldiers are threatening his right flank (later the officers realize the troops were from Jones' Confederate brigade returning from their failed attack near McLean's Ford).

VIGNETTE:
THE BLACK HORSE TROOP

When Jeb Stuart's squadron of the 1st Virginia cavalry charged into the 1st Minnesota and 11th New York, the soldiers misnamed these cavalrymen as the dreaded Black Horse Cavalry. In fact, in their memoirs, Union soldiers recalled seeing these Black Horsemen everywhere. Yet, at the time, there was only one company named the Black Horse Troop, and they belonged to the Thirtieth Virginia Battalion, commanded by Colonel Richard Radford and Lieutenant Colonel Thomas Munford.

In June 1859, the men of Warrenton (Fauquier County), Virginia, organized the cavalry company. Since most of their horses were black, they named themselves the Black Horse Troop. Its first service to Virginia and the United States came in December 1859. With the aid of the Mountain Rangers, a detachment of the Black Horse escorted John Brown through the streets of Charlestown, Virginia to his execution site outside the town.

At the outbreak of the War they became Confederate soldiers and accomplished their second assignment, capturing the U.S. armory at Harpers Ferry. During First Manassas, under the command of Captain William H. Payne, the Black Horse Troop harassed the Union artillerymen and infantrymen on the Warrenton Pike. While making one of their charges, a private from the Troop had his horse killed. The private fell, breaking his collar bone; yet, he sprang to his feet, ran after the Union infantryman, and fired his pistol, killing the man.

Altogether, the Thirtieth lost nine men killed and wounded, and at least six horses killed. They captured between sixty and eighty prisoners, fourteen pieces of artillery (including the big thirty-pounder cannon), thirty wagons, ambulances, and fifty horses.[4]

In the fall of 1861, they were made Company H of the 4th Virginia Cavalry.

Lieutenant Colonel Thomas Munford
30th Virginia battalion
(Seen in his brigadier general's uniform)

A drawing of a Black Horse cavalryman by Louisianan Leon J. Fremaux

VIGNETTE:
U.S. REPRESENTATIVE ALFRED ELY
"G——d d——n your white-livered soul"

Colonel E.B.C. Cash
8th South Carolina
(Postwar)

Captain E.P. Alexander
Engineer and Signal officer

Alfred Ely
U.S. Representative

Like many Northern civilians, Representative Alfred Ely, from Rochester, New York, was anxious to see the Confederate army routed. He had come from Washington earlier in the day to witness their defeat. Ignorant of the Union retreat, Ely remained close to the battlefield. In the late afternoon, two South Carolina officers approached him and asked for his name. The congressman answered, "Alfred Ely."

"What state are you from?"

"From the state of New York," Ely replied.

"Are you connected in any way with the government?"

"Yes."

"In what way, sir?"

"A Representative in Congress."

At this point the officers took him to their commander, Colonel Ellerbe Boggan Crawford Cash. "Colonel, this is Mr. Ely, Representative in Congress from New York," the officers reported.

The red-headed colonel became so angry that his face turned red and looked like a storm cloud. Confederate Captain E.P. Alexander described the scene:

> ...[Cash] *had drawn his revolver & was trying to shoot the little citizen who was dodging behind the big sergeant major as Cash turned his horse about & tried to get at him, poking at him with the pistol & swearing with a fluency which would have been creditable to a wagon master.*

*"You infernal s. of a b.! You came to see the fun did you?
God damn your dirty soul I'll show you," & he spurred
his horse to get around the sergeant major.*

*"What's the matter, Colonel," said I. "What are you try-
ing to shoot that man for?" "He's a member of Congress,
God damn him," said the colonel. "Came out here to see
the fun! Came to see us whipped & killed! God damn him!
If it was not for such as he there would be no war. They've
made it & then come to gloat over it! God damn him! I'll
show him," & again he tried to get at the poor little fellow
who was evidently scared almost into a fit. "But Colonel,"
I said, "you must not shoot a prisoner. Never shoot an un-
armed man."*[5]*

Cash refrained from murdering the congressman, and said to his
sergeant major, "...go & hunt the woods for Senator Foster. He is
hiding here somewhere. Go & find him, & God damn you, if you
bring him in alive I'll cut your ears off." Captain Alexander then
made Ely walk by his horse while he accompanied the congressman to the provost guard. Ely asked Alexander, "What sort of man
is Colonel Cash, sir?"

Alexander replied, "Well, you keep out of his way, or he would
as soon cut your ears off as not."[6]

The Confederates sent Ely to Richmond where he stayed a
prisoner of war for five months.

---

*Congressman Ely remembered Cash stating, "G——d d——n your white-livered soul! I'll blow
your brains out on the spot."[7]

Chapter 13

KILLED AND WOUNDED ───────────────

"I sat down by him and took a hearty cry..."

From Matthews Hill to Henry Hill the dead and mortally wounded, friend and foe alike, lay together. On Henry Hill a soldier from the 6th North Carolina counted forty dead horses in a space of fifty yards. The horses' and soldiers' bodies contaminated the streams and springs as they began to decompose in the summer heat.[1] With the conclusion of the battle, the Confederates were left with the task of burying the dead and caring for the wounded. Private John Opie, 5th Virginia, found

dead men in every conceivable position, mangled, dismembered, disemboweled—some torn literally to pieces. Some, in their death struggles, had torn up the ground around where they fell. Others had pulled up every weed or blade of grass that was in their reach. The horrible scene would have melted the heart of a demon...[2]

As the 1st Maryland (Confederate) reconnoitered the Chinn farm, Orderly Sergeant McHenry Howard sighted a Maine man propped against a tree. Approaching the man, Howard noted that the man's waist was terribly torn from an artillery shell. Howard expressed his sympathy and asked if he could do anything. The dying man pleaded, "You can do one thing for me, and I wish you to do it—for God's sake, take your bayonet and run me through, kill me at once and put an end to this." Howard refused but went to fetch water for the poor soldier. As he looked for a canteen he spotted a comrade who was preventing a wounded Union man from slitting his own throat. Sadly, these Confederates had time only to provide the wounded with warm, dirty water before they rejoined their units, leaving these Maine men to suffer a slow and agonizing death.[3]

It was a dreadful experience for these young men. For Private John Casler, 33d Virginia, the emotional strain overpowered him. While tracing the steps of his regiment's action he found his best friend, Private William I. Blue, lying dead face down near the Henry House.

...I turned him over to see where he was shot. He must have been shot through the heart, the place where he wanted to be shot, if shot at all. He must have been killed instantly, for he was in the act of loading his gun. One hand was grasped around his gun, in the other he held a cartridge, with one end of it in his mouth, in the act of tearing it off. I sat down by him and took a hearty cry, and then, thinks I, 'It does not look well for a soldier to cry,' but I could not help it.[4]

The harsh reality of war impressed their minds.

The Confederates dug long, shallow trenches for the Union dead, but buried their own comrades in individual graves with small markers, an unceremonious, unglamorous ending for these young Americans. And, that night, in almost Shakespearean fashion, a torrential downpour washed their blood from the fields.

McDowell reported nearly 500 killed, 1,000 wounded, 1,500 to 1,800 missing (presumed either dead, captured, or lost);[5] most of the Union missing had been captured. The Confederates counted 378 killed, 1,489 wounded, and 30 missing.[6]

**Sergeant McHenry
Howard, age 22**
1st Maryland

**Private John Opie,
age 17**
5th Virginia

**Private John Casler,
age 23**
33d Virginia

Chapter 14

SUMMARY

As Robert L. Wilson of Illinois walked with President Lincoln toward the White House he asked the president about the news from the battlefield. Lincoln politely stated he could not provide any information at that time due to military security. Wilson then inquired whether the news was good or bad. Lincoln grasped Wilson, placed his face near his ear, and in a shrill, subdued voice exclaimed, "It's damned bad!"[1]

At least eight factors contributed to the Confederate victory and the Union loss.

1) Union Major General Robert Patterson failed to detain Johnston's force in the Shenandoah Valley. From July 19–21 Johnston's force arrived at Manassas Junction and joined Beauregard's army; their combined forces numbered nearly 30,000. With these reinforcements the Confederates were only outnumbered by 5,000, and the generals quickly organized a mobile reserve.

2) McDowell's lingering for two days waiting for supplies around Centreville (July 19 and 20) also contributed to Union defeat. After the Blackburn's Ford skirmish he changed his attack plans—seeking now to turn the Confederate left flank. Yet, instead of using his cavalry to find a ford up stream, McDowell sent his chief engineer, Major John Barnard, with a few other officers to search for another crossing. It took this party two days, July 19 and 20, to locate another ford across Bull Run, and during these two days the majority of Johnston's force arrived in Manassas.

3) In addition to this delay, McDowell failed to productively utilize his entire force. His army numbered nearly 35,000; only 13,000–15,000 actually participated. He placed two divisions in reserve: Colonel Dixon Miles' 5th division (6,207) near Centreville and Brigadier General Theodore Runyon's 4th division (5,752) between Alexandria and Fairfax Court House, Virginia. Moreover, several regiments' three-month term expired, and those men left—about 700 or 800. Within the battle Richardson's brigade (3,920), Schenck's brigade (3,060) and half of Keyes' brigade (approximately 1,500) never played a significant role: Richardson stood idle near

Blackburn's Ford; Schenck's brigade never crossed the Stone Bridge, and Keyes used only two of his four regiments to assault Henry Hill. In all, more than 23,000 Union soldiers played little or no part in the day's fighting.

4) Poor logistics, and the sloppy execution of those plans, compounded the problem. First, he ordered Tyler's division to march at 2:30 a.m., July 21, and deploy two miles down the Warrenton Turnpike near the Stone Bridge. Yet, since Hunter's and Heintzelman's divisions constituted the primary attacking column and had the farthest route to cover (almost eight miles on small farm roads), they should have moved out first. Tyler took three and one-half hours to march two miles; and the flanking movement did not begin until 5:30 a.m., three hours behind schedule. To add to the delay the flanking column slowly trudged down the small farm road, removing felled trees and taking breaks from the summer heat. With this lagging the sun rose and the Confederates were able to observe the Union column. To meet this new threat, Colonel Evans ordered Wheat's Louisiana battalion and six companies from Sloan's 4th South Carolina toward Matthews Hill.

5) Union Brigade commander, Colonel Ambrose Burnside, threw his four regiments piecemeal into battle; it took nearly an hour before his entire brigade became involved. Colonel Andrew Porter's brigade, as well, slowly deployed on Burnside's right flank. Meanwhile, the Confederates rushed reinforcements into the area, and for an hour-and-a-half stubbornly stood their ground, buying time for more reinforcements to arrive.

6) Outnumbered, the Confederates finally retreated to Henry Hill. Yet, instead of pushing the attack, McDowell stopped for almost an hour-and-a-half in order to reorganize and regroup. (This time does not include Keyes' assault around 1:30 p.m.) Within this period, Jackson's brigade (2,412) arrived on Henry Hill and quickly established a defensive line. Including the disorganized brigades Beauregard estimated he had at this time 6,500 men. McDowell had nearly 13,000 men available.

7) Having rested and reorganized his men, McDowell ordered two batteries to Henry Hill. McDowell hoped to blow a hole in the Confederate line; then rush in the infantry to exploit the damage. This plan, however, failed miserably. At a range of only 300 yards the two sides dueled; the Confederate smoothbore cannon, more effective at shorter ranges, had a greater advantage over the Union rifled guns. Union artillery captain Griffin then redeployed two smoothbore howitzers dangerously close to the Confederate infantry line without Union infantry support. The 33d Virginia captured

these two guns, and a confusing whirlpool of determined charges and countercharges began.

8) Because McDowell mismanaged his divisions he only had fifteen regiments on hand to retake the eleven guns. Due to inexperienced officers and inadequate staff, he could not coordinate a full brigade-strength attack. At no time did more than two full regiments charge up the hill together, and because of the undisciplined nature of the regiments, many quickly dissolved into squads of men shooting haphazardly. With each assault the Confederates counterattacked and pushed the regiments back. (Although the Confederate regiments became disorganized and dishevelled, they were fighting on the defensive side and did not worry about a cohesive, tight formation.)

By 4:30 p.m., McDowell expended his fifteen regiments; the Confederates rushed reinforcements to the Chinn farm and Henry Hill area and overwhelmed the disorganized Union regiments. Due to poor Union generalship, undisciplined soldiers, and the quick reaction of many Confederate officers, the Confederacy won its first major battle at Manassas.*

---

*Some Confederates felt strongly that they should have pursued the Union troops to Washington, and captured the capital. In fact, officers later conjectured this was the closest the Confederates came in capturing the city and possibly ending the war. These officers, however, failed to appreciate the extreme disorganization of the Confederate army, and the fact that the men were tired, hungry, and nearly out of ammunition.

CHANGE OF COMMANDERS

"I have not lost a particle of confidence in you."

Two days after the battle Lincoln met with McDowell. Always polite, the president stated to the general, "I have not lost a particle of confidence in you."[1] The general, however, was unaware that the successful Union Major General George B. McClellan had been summoned to the White House. On Friday, July 26, Lincoln and his cabinet appointed McClellan commander of the Division of the Potomac.[2] On August 25, 1861, McClellan requested that no more Union regiments be uniformed in gray.[3] In addition, Congress organized a special congressional committee in December 1862, to review the failures and events of First Manassas, Ball's Bluff, Virginia and future battles. These hearings were recorded in the *Reports of Joint Committee on the Conduct of the War.*

McDowell's opponent as well was given a change of command. The day after the battle, Beauregard received a field promotion from President Jefferson Davis. Beauregard now boasted the title of full general. Yet, after he submitted his official report in August 1861, his relationship with Davis changed considerably. While giving special mention to his subordinate officers, the general credited himself for much of the victory. Furthermore, Beauregard stated that the Confederate War Department had rejected his plan for an offensive strategy at Manassas, implying that President Davis had not allowed him the authority to attack and defeat the Union army, and perhaps capture

Brigadier General McDowell and Major General McClellan

Washington, D.C. This angered Davis, and he wrote Beauregard saying the report seemed like "an attempt to exalt yourself at my expense."[4] The quarrel intensified in the following months. Finally, in January 1862, Beauregard accepted a transfer to the western theater. There he served under General Albert Sidney Johnston. Beauregard's next significant battle was Shiloh, Tennessee (April 6–7, 1862).

General Joseph E. Johnston remained commander of the Confederate army in Northern Virginia. On May 31, 1862, during the Battle of Seven Pines (Fair Oaks), a bullet struck him in the right shoulder and a shell fragment hit him in the chest, knocking him off his horse. It took six months for Johnston to recover from these wounds; he never again served with the Army of Northern Virginia. On June 1, 1862, General Robert Edward Lee assumed command of the Confederate army.[5]

Epilogue

First Manassas sparked a wide response throughout America and the world. The soldiers and commanders had faced the trauma of warfare; they had witnessed the death of their friends, and they had killed fellow Americans. Yet, as the regular officers previously advised, the volunteers needed more discipline, drilling, and better equipment.

To the Confederate soldiers their victory represented a conquest of a superior foe, successful defense of the Shenandoah Valley and Manassas, and a forced, humiliating retreat of the invading Union army back to Washington, D.C. Several Confederate officers thanked God; others accredited the win to hard fighting, persistence, and Southern domination. President Jefferson Davis, who arrived at the close of the battle, quickly wrote a note to the Confederate War Department:

> *Our forces have won a glorious victory...The enemy was routed and fled precipitously...Too high praise cannot be bestowed, whether for the skill of the principal officers or for the gallantry of all the troops."*[1]

Though some enthusiastic Confederates wished to pursue the Union army and capture the capital, Private Zettler, 8th Georgia, hoped the fighting was over. While walking among the dead he thought,

> *'Surely, surely, there will never be another battle.' It seemed...barbarous for men to try to settle any dispute or controversy by shooting one another, and, now that it had been realized what a battle meant, I felt sure there would never be another.*[2]

Many of the Union soldiers also had experienced enough fighting. The three-month enlistments were up, and one 69th New York officer boldly told his commander, Colonel Sherman, he was going home; he had served his three months, and the government had not paid him. Moreover, as a lawyer, he was neglecting his private practice and losing money. Sherman sharply replied, "You are a soldier, and must submit to orders till you are properly discharged. If you attempt to leave without orders, it will be mutiny, and I will shoot you like a dog!"[3] With a huff, the captain walked away but stayed within the camp. Later in the day, Lincoln addressed the 69th and offered to hear any grievances from the soldiers. This same man stepped forward and exclaimed, "...This morning I went to speak to Colonel Sherman, and he threatened to shoot me."

The president questioned the officer, "Threatened to shoot you?" Replying, the officer stated, "Yes, sir, he threatened to shoot me."

In a loud stage whisper, Lincoln replied, "Well, if I were you, and he threatened to shoot...I believe he would do it." The men laughed at their officer; embarrassed, he disappeared into the crowd.[4]

This spirit of mutiny was found throughout the Union army. To subdue this feeling the army sent several regiments to Fort Jefferson, Florida, as punishment. Other Union regiments recuperated from their losses, and began reorganizing and drilling every day. Yet, within a few days, the men faced "that terrible disease, camp diarrhoea [sic]." In some cases entire regiments suspended all duties. On August 1, 1861, however, the Union soldiers' morale lifted when the government paid them for one month and ten days' service. The amount totalled $15.03 in gold per man.[5]

While the soldiers rested, drilled, and combated camp diseases, the media reacted strongly to the events of July 21. The Richmond *Whig* arrogantly proclaimed, "The breakdown of the Yankee race, their unfitness for empire, forces dominion on the South. We are compelled to take the sceptre of power. We must adapt ourselves to our new destiny. We must elevate our race, every man of it, breed them up to arms, to command, to empire."[6] The New Orleans *Picayune* on July 23 printed:

> It is not the bulletins of our friend alone which announce a grand victory for the armies of the South. It is confessed in all its greatness and completeness by the wailings which come to us from the city of Washington, the head-quarters of our enemies. It is told in the groans of the panic-stricken Unionists of tyranny, who are quaking behind their entrenchments with apprehension for the approach of the avenging soldiery of the South,....From Richmond, on the contrary, come the glad signs of exceeding joy over a triumph of our arms, so great and overwhelming as though the God of Battles had fought visibly on our side, and smitten and scattered our enemies with a thunderbolt...We will not venture to say to what extent rage, disappointment, baffled cupidity, and thirst for revenge, may carry a deluded people; but the confidence of the South will rise high...[7]

In the North the naive thoughts of a quick victory and a reasonably bloodless war were shattered. Shock and dismay spread throughout the Northern population when they heard the tragic news; their powerful Northern army had been humiliated. Yet, once the initial surprise had sunk in, the North reacted with vengeful enthusiasm, and a second uprising occurred. The Providence *Journal* asked its readers:

> *What is to be done? Every thing. The capital must again be defended. The ground which has been lost, must be regained. Victory must follow on the heels of defeat. Not an inch more must be yielded. The ranks must be filled up. The fifty thousand must be made a hundred thousand. For every regiment that has been broken up, two must appear straightway. Let no man lisp the word discouragement. Let us begin to-day. Let not an hour be lost. Let the Government say when and whence it wants men, and they shall be forthcoming. Such at least is the spirit of Rhode Island.*[8]

Throughout the North the newspapers resounded with these same sentiments.

Europe was also watching. Observing America's reaction, the London *Daily News* predicted, "The grand controversy between the North and the South has at length reached the point it has been for years past gradually approaching—the *ultima ratio* of force; and the sword having now been drawn in earnest, it must be fought out."[9]

Neither side would admit defeat; a clear victory and a complete submission must be won. Sadly, Private Zettler's wish for no further battles would not come true. For the next four years thousands of Americans would meet again and again, staining fields of battle with their crimson blood.

SPOILS OF WAR

Several weeks after the battle the Confederate Ordnance Department released a list of captured goods:

One 30-pounder Parrott gun, with 300 rounds of ammunition;

28 field pieces with 100 rounds of ammunition each;

37 caissons;

6 traveling forging wagons;

4 battery wagons, fully equipped;

64 artillery horses with harness;

500,000 rounds of small arms ammunition;

4,500 sets of accouterments;

over 500 muskets;

9 regimental and garrison flags;

an abundance of pistols, knapsacks, swords, canteens, blankets, axes, intrenching tools, wagons, ambulances, horses, camp and garrison equipment, hospital stores and some food. In addition, 1,600 prisoners were captured: 3 colonels: Colonel Orlando Willcox, brigade commander in Colonel Samuel P. Heintzelman's division, Colonel Michael Corcoran, 69th New York and Colonel A.M. Wood, 14th Brooklyn; 1 major, 13 captains, 36 lieutenants, 2 quartermasters, 5 surgeons, 7 assistant surgeons, 2 chaplains, 15 citizens and 1,376 enlisted men.[1]

STATES REPRESENTED AT FIRST MANASSAS AND THEIR KILLED AND WOUNDED _____

CONFEDERATE

Alabama: 40 killed; 156 wounded

Georgia: 60 killed; 293 wounded

Louisiana: 11 killed; 58 wounded

Maryland: 1 killed; 5 wounded

Mississippi: 43 killed; 147 wounded

North Carolina: 24 killed; 53 wounded

South Carolina: 44 killed; 268 wounded

Tennessee: 1 killed; 3 wounded

Virginia: 174 killed; 579 wounded*

UNION

Connecticut: 6 killed; 26 wounded

Maine: 57 killed; 118 wounded

Massachusetts: 14 killed; 67 wounded

Michigan: 6 killed; 37 wounded

Minnesota: 42 killed; 108 wounded

New Hampshire: 9 killed; 35 wounded

New Jersey: rear-guard—no casualties

New York: 236 killed; 449 wounded†

Ohio: 2 killed; 6 wounded

Rhode Island: 38 killed; 102 wounded

Vermont: 6 killed; 22 wounded

Wisconsin: 24 killed; 65 wounded

U.S. Artillery: 22 killed; 39 wounded

U.S. Cavalry: 13 wounded

U.S. Infantry: 10 killed; 20 wounded

U.S. Marine: 9 killed; 19 wounded

*Suffered the highest casualties of any state—753.
†Second highest casualties of any state—685.

ORDER OF BATTLES

CONFEDERATE

Army of the Potomac
Brigadier General P.G.T. Beauregard

Brigadier General Milledge L. Bonham First Brigade	K	W	M
Colonel William K. Kirkland 11th North Carolina	—	—	—
Colonel Joseph B. Kershaw 2d South Carolina	6	43	—
Colonel J.H. Williams 3d South Carolina	—	—	—
Colonel Thomas G. Bacon 7th South Carolina	—	—	—
Colonel Ellerbe Boggan Crawford Cash 8th South Carolina	5	23	—
Attached Units			
Colonel H.B. Kelly 8th Louisiana			
Colonel Richard C.W. Radford 30th Virginia Cavalry	5	4	—
Captain Del Kemper Alexandria Light Artillery (4 guns)	1	2	—
Captain John Shields 1st Company, Richmond Howitzers (4 guns)			

K= Killed
W= Wounded
M= Missing
C= Captured

Brigadier General Richard S. Ewell
Second Brigade (Not Actively Engaged)

Colonel Robert E. Rodes
5th Alabama

Colonel John J. Seibels
6th Alabama

Colonel J.G. Seymour
6th Louisiana

Attached Units

Lieutenant Thomas L. Rosser
Washington Artillery (4 guns)

Lieutenant Colonel Walter H. Jenifer
Cavalry Battalion

Brigadier General David R. Jones

Third Brigade	K	W	M
Colonel W.S. Featherston 17th Mississippi	2	10	—
Colonel E.R. Burt 18th Mississippi	9	29	—
Colonel M. Jenkins 5th South Carolina	3	23	—

Attached Units

Captain J.W. Flood
Flood's Company, 30th Virginia Cavalry

Captain M.B. Miller
Washington Artillery (2 guns)

Brigadier General James Longstreet

Fourth Brigade			
Colonel Joseph P. Jones 5th North Carolina	1	3	—
Major Frederick G. Skinner 1st Virginia	—	6	—
Colonel Samuel Garland, Jr. 11th Virginia	—	—	—
Colonel Montgomery Dent Corse 17th Virginia	1	3	—
Colonel Peter Hariston 24th Virginia			

Attached Units

Lieutenant John J. Garnett
Washington Artillery (2 guns)

Captain Edgar Whitehead
Company E, 30th Virginia Cavalry

Colonel P. St. George Cocke
Fifth Brigade

	K	**W**	**M**
Colonel Eppa Hunton 8th Virginia	6	23	—
Colonel Robert E. Withers 18th Virginia	6	13	—
Lieutenant Colonel James Bowie Strange 19th Virginia	1	4	—
Colonel Robert T. Preston 28th Virginia	—	9	—
Colonel William Smith 49th Virginia Infantry Battalion	10	30	—

Attached Units

Captain Arthur Lee Rogers
Loudoun Artillery (4 guns)　　　— 　　3 　　—

Captain Henry G. Latham
Lynchburg Artillery (4 guns)

Colonel Jubal A. Early
Sixth Brigade

Colonel Harry T. Hays 7th Louisiana	3	20	—
Colonel William Barksdale 13th Mississippi	—	6	—
Colonel John L. Kemper 7th Virginia	9	38	—

Attached Unit

Lieutenant C.W. Squires
Lieutenant J.B. Richardson
Lieutenant J.B. Whittington
Washington Artillery (5 guns)

Colonel Nathan G. Evans

Seventh Brigade	K	W	M
Major C.R. Wheat (W)			
1st Special Louisiana Infantry Battalion	8	38	—
Colonel J.B.E. Sloan			
4th South Carolina	11	79	6

Attached Units

Captain J.D. Alexander
    Alexander's Troop, 30th Virginia Cavalry

Captain W.R. Terry
    Terry's Troop, 30th Virginia Cavalry

Reserve Brigade (Not Engaged)

Brigadier General Theophilus H. Holmes

Colonel J.F. Fagan
    1st Arkansas

Colonel W. Bate
    2d Tennessee

Attached Unit

Captain L. Walker
    Purcell Artillery (6 guns)

Unbrigaded Units

	K	W	M
Colonel Wade Hampton (W)			
Hampton's South Carolina Legion	19	100	2
Camp Pickens Battery (15 guns)			

Army of the Shenandoah
General Joseph E. Johnston

Brigadier General Thomas J. Jackson

First Brigade	K	W	M
Colonel James W. Allen			
2d Virginia	18	72	—
Colonel James F. Preston			
4th Virginia	31	100	—
Colonel Kenton Harper			
5th Virginia	6	47	—

	K	**W**	**M**
Lieutenant Colonel John Echols 27th Virginia	19	122	—
Colonel Arthur C. Cummings 33d Virginia (8 companies)	45	101	—

Attached Unit

Rockbridge Virginia Artillery (4 guns)

Colonel Francis Bartow (K)
Second Brigade

	K	**W**	**M**
Colonel Lucius J. Gartell 7th Georgia	19	134	—
Lieutenant Colonel William M. Gardner 8th Georgia	41	159	—

Attached Unit

Captain Ephriam G. Alburtis
Wise Artillery (Alburtis's battery, 4 guns)

Brigadier General Barnard Bee (M.W.)
Third Brigade

	K	**W**	**M**
Colonel Egbert Jones (M.W.) 4th Alabama	40	156	—
Colonel W.C. Falkner 2d Mississippi	25	81	1
Lieutenant Colonel Philip F. Liddell 11th Mississippi (2 companies)	7	21	—
Colonel Charles F. Fisher (K) 6th North Carolina	23	50	—

Attached Unit

Captain John Imboden
Staunton Artillery (4 guns)

Colonel Arnold Elzey
Fourth Brigade

	K	**W**	**M**
Lieutenant Colonel George H. Steuart 1st Maryland Infantry Battalion	1	5	—
Colonel John C. Vaughn 3d Tennessee	1	3	—
Colonel Simeon B. Gibbons 10th Virginia	6	10	—

Attached Unit

Lieutenant R.F. Beckham
    Culpeper Artillery (4 guns)

Unbrigaded Units

Colonel James Ewell Brown Stuart
    1st Virginia Cavalry

Captain Philip B. Stanard
    Stanard's Artillery (4 guns)

UNION

Army of Northeastern Virginia
Brigadier General Irvin McDowell

Brigadier General Daniel Tyler
First Division

Colonel Erasmus Keyes **First Brigade**	**K**	**W**	**M**
Colonel Charles D. Jameson 2d Maine	13	24	118
Lieutenant Colonel John Speidel 1st Connecticut	—	8	9
Colonel Alfred H. Terry 2d Connecticut	2	5	9
Colonel John L. Chatfield 3d Connecticut	4	13	18

Brigadier General Robert C. Schenck
Second Brigade

Colonel George W.B. Tompkins 2d New York	19	15	36
Colonel A. McD. McCook 1st Ohio	1	4	7
Lieutenant Colonel Rodney Mason 2d Ohio	1	2	8

Attached Unit

Captain J. Howard Carlisle Company E, 2d U.S. Artillery (7 guns)	—	4	11

Colonel William T. Sherman
Third Brigade

	K	W	M
Colonel Isaac F. Quinby 13th New York	11	27	20
Colonel Michael Corcoran (W&C); Captain James Kelly 69th New York	38	59	95
Colonel James Cameron (K) 79th New York	32	51	115
Lieutenant Colonel Harry W. Peck 2d Wisconsin	24	65	23

Attached Unit

	K	W	M
Captain Romeyn B. Ayres Company E, 5th U.S. Artillery (6 guns)	4	2	—

Colonel Israel B. Richardson
Fourth Brigade
(Casualties for July 18)

	K	W	M
Colonel R. Cowdin 1st Massachusetts	10	8	14
Colonel Ezra L. Walrath 12th New York	5	19	10
Major A.W. Williams 2d Michigan	—	1	—
Colonel Daniel McConnell 3d Michigan	—	1	—

Attached Units

Lieutenant John Edwards
Company G, 1st U.S. Artillery (2 guns)

Captain Henry J. Hunt
Company M, 2d U.S. Artillery (4 guns)

Colonel David Hunter (W)
Colonel Andrew Porter
Second Division

Colonel Andrew Porter
Adjutant William Averell

First Brigade	**K**	**W**	**M**
Colonel George Lyons			
8th New York (Militia)	8	17	13
Colonel Alfred M. Wood (W&C);			
Lieutenant Colonel E.B. Fowler			
14th Brooklyn	23	48	71
Colonel Henry W. Slocum (W);			
Major Joseph J. Bartlett			
27th New York	26	44	60
Major George Sykes			
U.S. Infantry Battalion (8 companies)	10	20	53
Major John G. Reynolds			
U.S. Marine Corps Battalion	9	19	16

Attached Units

Major Innis N. Palmer			
U.S. Cavalry Battalion (7 companies)	—	13	—
Captain Charles Griffin			
Company D, 5th Artillery (6 guns)	4	13	10

Colonel Ambrose E. Burnside
Second Brigade

Colonel Gilman Marston (W);			
Lieutenant Colonel Frank S. Fiske			
2d New Hampshire	9	35	63
Major Joseph P. Balch			
1st Rhode Island	13	39	39
Colonel John S. Slocum (K);			
Lieutenant Colonel Frank Wheaton			
2d Rhode Island	23	49	—
Colonel Henry P. Martin			
71st New York (Militia)	10	40	12

Attached Unit

Captain William Reynolds
Reynolds' Rhode Island Battery (6 guns)

Colonel Samuel P. Heintzelman (W)
Third Division

Colonel William Franklin
First Brigade

	K	**W**	**M**
Colonel Samuel C. Lawrence (W) 5th Massachusetts	5	26	28
Colonel George Clark, Jr. 11th Massachusetts	8	40	40
Colonel Willis A. Gorman 1st Minnesota	42	108	30

Attached Unit

Captain James B. Ricketts Company I, 1st U.S. Artillery (6 guns)	12	15	—

Colonel Orlando B. Willcox (W&C);
Colonel J.H. Hobart Ward
Second Brigade

Colonel Noah Farnham (M.W.) 11th New York	48	75	65
Colonel J.H. Hobart Ward; Lieutenant Colonel Addison Farnsworth 38th New York	15	55	58
Major Alonzo F. Bidwell 1st Michigan	6	37	70
Colonel D.A. Woodbury 4th Michigan (Not engaged)	—	—	—

Attached Unit

Captain Richard Arnold Company D, 2d U.S. Artillery (4 guns)	2	5	3

Colonel Oliver O. Howard
Third Brigade

Major Henry G. Staples 3d Maine	5	8	74
Colonel Hiram G. Berry 4th Maine	26	46	121
Colonel Mark H. Dunnell 5th Maine	13	40	335
Colonel Henry Whiting 2d Vermont	6	22	92

Brigadier General Theodore Runyon
Fourth Division
(Held in reserve, not actively engaged.)

Militia: Colonel A.J. Johnson
1st New Jersey

Colonel H.M. Baker
3d New Jersey

Colonel W. Napton
3d New Jersey

Colonel M. Miller
4th New Jersey

Volunteers: Colonel W.R. Montgomery
1st New Jersey

Colonel G.W. McClean
2d New Jersey

Colonel G.W. McClean
3d New Jersey

Colonel L. Von Gilsa
41st New York

Colonel Dixon S. Miles
Fifth Division

Colonel Louis Blenker
First Brigade

	K	W	M
Lieutenant Colonel J. Stahel 8th New York (Volunteers)	2	2	7
Colonel A. Von Steinwehr 29th New York	2	9	35
Colonel F.G. D'Utassy 39th New York	2	5	54
Colonel M. Einstein 27th Pennsylvania	—	—	—

Attached Units

	K	W	M
Captain J.C. Tidball Company A, 2d U.S. Artillery (4 guns)	—	—	—
Captain C. Brookwood Brookwood's New York Battery (6 guns)	—	—	—

Colonel Thomas A. Davies
Second Brigade

	K	W	M
Lieutenant Colonel S. Marsh 16th New York	—	1	1
Colonel W.A. Jackson 18th New York	—	—	—
Colonel C.E. Pratt 31st New York	—	1	1

	K	**W**	**M**
Colonel R. Matheson 32d New York	—	—	—

Attached Unit

| Lieutenant O.D. Greene
    Company G, 2d U.S. Artillery (4 guns) | — | — | — |

TOUR OF MANASSAS NATIONAL BATTLEFIELD PARK

For those who are planning to visit the Manassas National Battlefield Park a suggested tour is listed. (Note, these stops are not listed at the battle site.)

NOTES

Introduction

1. This number only indicates the men actively involved in the battle. McDowell engaged about 13,000–15,000 soldiers out of his 35,000-man army. The Confederates countered McDowell's attack with approximately 14,650. See Robert M. Johnston, *Bull Run: Its Strategies and Tactics* (New York: Houghton Mifflin Company, 1913), pp. 266–67.

2. Grady McWhiney and Perry D. Jamieson, *Attack and Die: Civil War Military Tactics and the Southern Heritage* (Tuscaloosa: The University of Alabama Press, 1982), p. 40.

Chapter 1

1. Ulysses S. Grant, *Personal Memoirs of U.S. Grant* (New York: Da Capo, 1982), p. 44.

2. The information in this chapter was developed from an interview with Mr. Jim Burgess, November 9, 1995. Mr. Burgess is the Manassas Museum Technician. For the past twenty years he has been firing black powder weapons in competitions and is considered a marksman and expert on 19th-century weaponry. See also Jack Coggins, *Arms and Equipment of the Civil War.* Garden City, New York: Doubleday and Company, Inc., 1962.

3. Terry L. Jones, *Lee's Tigers: The Louisiana Infantry in the Army of Northern Virginia* (Baton Rouge: Louisiana State University Press, 1952), p. 4. Blue jackets were discovered to be worn by the Tiger Rifles when several Tigers' bodies were recently exhumed.

4. McHenry Howard, *Recollections of a Maryland Confederate Soldier and Staff Officer* (Baltimore: Williams and Wilkins Co., 1914), pp. 9–10.

5. Mark M. Boatner III, *The Civil War Dictionary* (New York: Vintage Books, 1991), p. 954. See also, Frederick P. Todd, *American Military Equipage 1851–1872* (Providence: The Company of Military Historians, 1974), pp. 45–50; Harrison H. Comings, *Personal Reminiscences of Company E, New York Fire Zouaves, Better Known As Ellsworth's Fire Zouaves* (Malden, Massachusetts: J. Gould Tilden, Steam Book, 1886), p. 8. Comings' account can be found at the Military History Institute's Archives Division, Carlisle, Pennsylvania.

6. Comings, p. 8; "The Fire Zouaves," Chapt. XLII, in *Our Firemen*, p. 730. Both can be found in the Archives Division of the Military History Institute, Carlisle, Pennsylvania; Frederick P. Todd, *American Military Equipage 1851–1872*, "State Forces,"* vol. II (Chatham Square Press, Inc., 1983), p. 1047. *The Soldier In Our Civil War: A Pictorial History of the Conflict, 1861–1865*, vol. I (New York: J.H. Brown Pub. Co., 1884), p. 73.

7. C. Tevis, *The History of the Fighting Fourteenth* (Baltimore: Butternut and Blue, 1993), p. 25; Todd, *"State Forces,"* vol. II, p. 1041.

8. Warren H. Cudworth, *History of the First Regiment (Massachusetts Infantry)* (Boston: Walker, Fuller, and Company, 1866), pp. 42–44. Gustavus B. Hutchinson, *A Narrative of the Formation and Services of the Eleventh Massachusetts Volunteers, From April 15, 1861, to July 14, 1865* (Boston: Alfred Mudge

and Son, 1893), p. 22. William T. Sherman, *Memoirs of General William T. Sherman* (New York: Da Capo Press, 1984), p. 184. Charles B. Fairchild, *History of the 27th Regiment N.Y. Vols* (Binghamton: Carl and Matthews, 1888), p. 12. Martin Haynes, *A History of the Second Regiment, New Hampshire Volunteer Infantry* (Lakeport, New Hampshire: 1896), p. 7.

9. Elisha Hunt Rhodes, *All For the Union: The Civil War Diary and Letters of Elisha Hunt Rhodes*, ed. Robert Hunt Rhodes (New York: Orion Books, 1985), p. 15.

10. William Todd, *The Seventy-Ninth Highlanders* (Albany: Brandow, Barton and Co., 1886), p. 18.

11. Dennis E. Frye, *2nd Virginia Infantry* (Lynchburg: H.E. Howard, 1984), p. 8.

12. Frederick P. Todd, *American Military Equipage*, "The United States Army," Part I, vol. II,

13. Joseph H. Crute, Jr., *Emblems of Southern Valor: The Battle Flags of the Confederacy* (Louisville: Harmony House, 1990), p. 13.

14. George Henry Preble, *History of the Flag of the United States of America* (Boston: James R. Osgood and Company, 1882), pp. 511–24.

15. Douglas Southall Freeman, *Lee's Lieutenants: A Study in Command*, vol. I (New York: Charles Scribner's Sons, 1942), p. 6.

16. T. Harry Williams, *P.G.T. Beauregard: Napoleon in Gray* (Baton Rouge: Louisiana State University Press, 1955), pp. 49–50.

17. Boatner III, p. 441. Freeman, vol. I, p. 111. See also *The War of the Rebellion: A Compilation of the Official Records of the Union and Confederate Armies*, ser. I, vol. II (Washington, D.C.: Government Printing Office, 1880–1901), pp. 471–72. Cited hereafter as O.R.

18. Williams, *Lincoln and His Generals* (New York: Vintage Books, 1952), p. 19. Boatner, p. 530. And, Ezra J. Warner, *Generals in Blue* (Baton Rouge: Louisiana State University Press, 1964), pp. 297–98.

19. All information found in the captions in the section "Organization of the Armies" can be found in Warner, *Generals in Blue*; Ezra J. Warner's, *Generals in Gray* (Baton Rouge: Louisiana State University Press, 1959); Boatner III, *The Civil War Dictionary*; Brevet Major General George W. Cullum's, *Biographical Register of the Officers and Graduates of the U.S. Military Academy At West Point, N.Y. From Its Establishment, In 1802, To 1890 With the early History of the United States Military Academy*, 3d ed., vol. I (New York: Houghton, Mifflin and Company, 1891). For specific information on Colonel Nathan Evans (CSA) see, G. Moxley Sorrel, *Recollections of a Confederate Staff Officer* (New York: The Neale Publishing Co., 1905), p. 93.

20. The figures in this section can be found in Johnston's, *Bull Run: Its Strategy and Tactics*, pp. 109–10.

21. Ibid., p. 267.

22. P.G.T. Beauregard, "The First Battle of Bull Run," *Battles and Leaders of The Civil War*, eds. Robert U. Johnson and Clarence C. Buel (New York: Castle, 1888), vol. I , p. 196. Cited hereafter as *B&L*. Williams, *P.G.T. Beauregard*, p. 70.

23. O.R., vol. II, p. 485; Freeman, pp. 42–43; Williams, *P.G.T. Beauregard*, pp. 70–73.

24. O.R., vol. II, p. 168.

25. William C. Davis, *First Blood: Fort Sumter to Bull Run* (Alexandria: Time Life Books, 1983), p. 119. See also, Civil War Letters Collection, Chicago Historical Society.

26. "The Dead Behead Easily," *First Manassas (Bull Run) and the war around it...* (Manassas, Virginia: First Manassas Corporation, 1961), pp. 34–37, 59. See

also "Documents," *The Rebellion Record*, vol. 4., pp. 535–36 & *Gray Ghosts and Rebel Raiders* (New York: Holt, Rinehart and Winston), 1957.

27. Haynes, p. 20.
28. Todd, *The Seventy-Ninth Highlanders*, p. 19.
29. Ibid., pp. 20–21.
30. Ibid., p. 19.

Chapter 2

1. O.R., vol. II, p. 312.
2. Ibid., p. 311.
3. Cudworth, pp. 42–43.
4. William H. Morgan, *Personal Reminiscences of the War of 1861–1865* (Lynchburg: Virginia, J.P. Bell Company, Inc., 1911), pp. 53–54.
5. O.R., vol. II, p. 313.
6. John J. Hennessy, *The First Battle of Manassas: An End To Innocence July 18–21 1861* (Lynchburg, Virginia: H.E. Howard, Inc., 1989), p. 20.
7. O.R., vol. II, p. 313.
8. Morgan, pp. 57–58.
9. O.R., vol. II, p. 313.
10. William M. Owen, *In Camp and Battle with the Washington Artillery of New Orleans* (Boston: Ticknor and Company, 1885), p. 28. And, O.R., vol. II, p. 311.
11. O.R., vol. II, pp. 314, 462.
12. Scott Hart, "Wilmer McLean...he would study war no more," *First Manassas (Bull Run) and the war around it...* (Manassas, Virginia: First Manassas Corporation, 1961), pp. 51–52, 62.

Chapter 3

1. Hart, pp. 330–31.
2. Ibid., p. 318.
3. O.R., vol. II, p. 487. Beauregard stated in *B&L*, vol. I, p. 202; 29,188 infantrymen and 55 guns.
4. *B&L*, vol. I, p. 205.
5. O.R., vol. II, p. 487.

Chapter 4

1. George M. Finch, "Boys of '61." *G.A.R. Papers*, vol. I (Cincinnati: Fred C. Jones Post, 1891), p. 255.
2. General Peter C. Hains, "The First Gun at Bull Run," *Cosmopolitan Magazine*, vol. 51 (1911), pp. 388–91. See also Alan D. Gaff, *If this is War: A History of the Campaign of Bull's Run by the Wisconsin Regiment Thereafter Known as the Ragged Ass Second* (Dayton, Ohio: Morningside, 1991), p. 187.
3. O.R., vol. II, p. 559. See also, Charles L. Dufour, *Gentle Tiger: The Gallant Life of Roberdeau Wheat* (Baton Rouge: Louisiana State University Press, 1957), p. 134.
4. O.R., vol. II, p. 348.
5. Finch, p. 256.
6. Edward Porter Alexander, *Fighting for the Confederacy: The Personal Recollections of General Edward Porter Alexander*, ed. Gary W. Gallagher (Chapel Hill: The University of North Carolina Press, 1989), p. 50.

Chapter 5

1. George A. Otis and D.L. Huntington, *The Medical and Surgical History of the War of the Rebellion*, part 3, vol. II (Washington: Government Printing Office, 1883), p. 6.
2. Augustus Woodbury, *The Second Rhode Island Regiment: A Narrative of Military Operations* (Providence, 1873), p. 31.
3. Rhodes, p. 26.
4. Lieutenant Colonel Francis S. Fiske, "Second New Hampshire Regiment at Bull Run," n.p., n.d. Found in the U.S. Military History Institute's library, Carlisle, Pennsylvania.
5. Hennessy, pp. 49–50.
6. Fiske, p. 156.

Chapter 6

1. See Manassas Park Pamphlet given out at the Stone House.

   Since Burnside's brigade fought only on Matthews Hill his casualties are considered in this section. Porter's brigade casualties are counted in the Young's Branch area and on Henry Hill. Although the Confederate regiments—Evans' (Wheat's battalion and 4th South Carolina), Bee's (4th Alabama, 2d and 11th Mississippi), Bartow's (7th and 8th Georgia)—battled on Henry Hill, their heaviest losses were on Matthews Hill and Young's Branch area. Consequently, their casualty list is figured for Matthews Hill.
2. Thomas M. Aldrich, *The History of Battery A: First Regiment Rhode Island Light Artillery in the War to Preserve the Union: 1861–1865* (Providence: Snow and Farnham, 1904), p. 19.
3. Rhodes, p. 33.
4. Jones, p. 51.
5. Aldrich, p. 20.
6. Rhodes, pp. 27–28. See also, Woodbury, *The Second Rhode Island*, p. 34.
7. Jones, p. 52. See also, Dufour, p. 138 and Horace H. Cunningham, *Field Medical Services at the Battles of Manassas (Bull Run)* (Athens, Georgia: University of Georgia Press, 1968), p. 28.
8. Gregory J. Starbuck, "Up Alabamians!" The 4th Alabama Infantry at First Manassas. *Military Images*. July–August 1986. For the second rendition of Bee's orders see Major Richard Watson York's article, "The 'Old Third' Brigade and the Death of General Bee," *Our Living and Our Dead; Devoted to North Carolina—Her Past, Her Present and Her Future*, vol. I, Sept. 1874 to Feb. 1875 (Raleigh: Southern Historical Society), p. 563.
9. Hennessy, p. 56.
10. For the account of the battle in the cornfield see, Starbuck, p. 27; for the wounds concerning Lieutenant Colonel Law and Major Scott see, R.T. Coles, *From Huntsville to Appomattox: R.T. Coles's History of 4th Regiment, Alabama Volunteer Infantry, C.S.A., Army of Northern Virginia*, ed. Jeffrey D. Stocker (Knoxville: The University of Tennessee Press, 1996), pp. 226, endnote 17 and 238, endnote 39.
11. Starbuck, p. 27.
12. Information within these captions can be found in Coles, pp. 224 and 229.
13. Alice V.D. Pierrepont, *Reuben Vaughan Kidd: Soldier of the Confederacy* (Petersburg: Violet Bank, 1947), p. 294.
14. Ibid.

15. O.R., vol. II, p. 487. Contemporary accounts have placed the 7th Georgia on Matthews Hill. The primary sources, however, contradict this view. See R.C. M'Daniel's, Co. G, 7th Ga, article in *Atlantic Monthly*, February 23, 1901; Sergeant W.O. Hudson's, 4th Alabama, letter in *Our Living and Our Dead; Devoted to North Carolina—Her Past, Her Present and Her Future*, vol. I, p. 563. Hudson specifically remembered that the 8th Georgia deployed to the right of the 4th Alabama. See also, T.B. Warder and Jas. M. Catlett. *Battle of Young's Branch or Manassas Plain* (Richmond: Enquirer Book and Job Press, 1862).

16. Berrien M. Zettler, *War Stories and School-Day Incidents: For the Children* (New York: Neale Publishing Co., 1912), pp. 62–64.

17. Ibid., p. 64.

18. Fiske, p. 157.

19. Ibid., p. 66.

20. *Savannah Republican*, August 1, 1861. Zettler, p. 66.

21. Hennessy, pp. 57–58.

22. William W. Averell, *Ten Years in the Saddle: The Memoirs of William Woods Averell*, eds. Edward K. Eckert and Nicholas J. Amato (San Rafael: Presidio Press, 1978), p. 297.

23. Sykes' battalion consisted of two companies of Second U.S. Infantry, five companies of the Third U.S. Infantry, and one company of the Eighth Infantry, O.R., vol. II, p. 390.

24. Capt. Robert G. Carter, *Four Brothers In Blue or Sunshine and Shadows of the War of the Rebellion: A Story of the Great Civil War from Bull Run to Appomattox* (Austin: University of Texas Press, 1913), p. 13.

25. Edward Porter Alexander, "The Battle of Bull Run," *Scribners Magazine*, vol. XLI (1907), p. 89.

26. Beauregard, *B&L*, vol. I, p. 210.

Chapter 7

1. Beuregard, *B&L*, vol. I, , pp. 13–15.

2. Brigadier General John D. Imboden, "Incidents of the First Bull Run," *B&L*, vol. I, p. 233.

3. John Coxe, "The Battle of First Manassas," *Confederate Veteran* (Nashville, Tennessee) vol. XXIII, No. 1, January 1915, pp. 25–26. See also, T.B. Warder and Jas. M. Catlett, pp. 38, 47–49.

4. Averell, p. 298.

5. Fairchild, pp. 12–13. Private Wesley Randall, of Binghamton, New York, was the first man killed in the 27th New York.

6. Ibid., p. 13.

7. Coxe, p. 26.

8. Her exploits as a soldier and a Confederate spy can be found in her book, *The Woman in Battle: A Narrative of the Exploits, Adventures and Travels of Madame Loreta Janeta Velazquez, Otherwise Known As, Lieutenant Harry T. Buford*, ed. C.J. Worthington (Hartford: T. Belknap, 1876), p. 102.

Chapter 8

1. Imboden, *B&L*, vol. I, p. 234.

2. Lieutenant Colonel G.F.R. Henderson, *Stonewall Jackson and the American Civil War*, vol. I (Secaucus, New Jersey: Blue and Grey), p. 145.

3. Hennessy, p. 69.

4. O.R., vol. II, p. 187.

5. Jackson adopted this reverse slope tactic from the Duke of Wellington (Arthur Welleseley), who effectively used this tactic in several of his battles, see Henderson, p. 146.

6. Beauregard, *B&L*, vol. I, p. 211. See also Hennessy, p. 71.

7. *B&L*, vol. I, p. 211.

8. Brevet Major General James B. Fry, "McDowell's Advance to Bull Run," *B&L*, vol. I.

9. Sherman, p. 183. Sherman was able to quickly span Bull Run because earlier in the day he saw a Confederate horseman cross the stream. He kept a mental note of where he had seen this crossing and traversed at this same point.

10. Ibid., p. 188.

11. Todd, *Seventy-Ninth Highlanders*, p. 34. See also, Henry N. Blake, *Three Years In the Army of the Potomac* (Boston: Lee and Shepard, 1865), p. 16.

12. Hennessy, p. 74.

Chapter 9

1. O.R., vol. II, p. 353.

2. James H. Mundy, *Second to None: The Story of the 2d. Maine Volunteers "The Bangor Regiment"* (Scarborough, Maine: Harp Publications, 1992), pp. 70–71. See also O.R., vol. II, p. 353.

3. Ibid., pp. 66–67.

4. William C. Davis, *Battle at Bull Run: A History of the First Major Campaign of the Civil War* (Garden City, New York: Doubleday and Company, Inc., 1977), p. 233. For the "Yankee Yell" see R.L.T. Beale, *History of the Ninth Virginia Cavalry in the War Between the States* (Richmond: B.F. Johnson Publishing Co., 1899), p. 191.

5. O.R., vol. II, p. 567. See also Hennessy, p. 75.

6. O.R., vol. II, p. 353. For information concerning the 2d Maine see Mundy, pp. 73–75.

7. *Report of the Joint Committee on the Conduct of the War, In Three Parts: Bull Run to Ball's Bluff*, Part II (Washington: Government Printing Office, 1863), p. 169. Hereafter cited *CCW*.

8. Ibid., p. 243.

9. *B&L*, p. 234. Helena Huntington Smith, "At the Eye of the Hurricane," *First Manassas (Bull Run) and the war around it....* (Manassas: First Manassas Corporation, 1961), pp. 19–20, 57–59. See also Joseph Mills Hanson, *Bull Run Remembers...The History, Traditions and Landmarks of the Manassas (Bull Run) Campaigns Before Washington 1861–1862* (Manassas: National Capitol Publisher, Inc., 1953), pp. 88–89 and Hennessy, p. 79. Hanson's account differs with Smith's. He states Rosa Stokes was Mrs. Henry's maid and that Rosa was wounded in the ankle.

10. *CCW*, p. 220.

11. Ibid., p. 219.

12. James I. Robertson, Jr., *The Stonewall Brigade* (Baton Rouge: Louisiana State University Press, 1963), p. 38. See also J.B. Caddall, 4th Regiment, in *Richmond Times-Dispatch*, November 27, 1904.

13. Henderson, p. 147.

14. John O. Casler, *Four Years in the Stonewall Brigade* (Girard, Kansas: Appeal Publishing Co., 1906), p. 27. Casler was born in Gainsboro, Virginia. His family moved to Springfield, Virginia. In 1859, he moved to Sedalia, Missouri, but returned to Virginia in April 1861.

15. Hennessy, p. 80.

16. Private Lewis Herbert Metcalf, "So Eager Were We All..." *American Heritage*, vol. XVI, no. 4 (June 1965), p. 37.

17. Harrison H. Comings, *Personal Reminiscences of Company E, New York Fire Zouaves, Bettter Known As Ellsworth's Fire Zouaves*. Found at U.S. Military History Institute, Archives Division, Carlisle, Pennsylvania.

18. Sergeant John G. Merritt, "A Minnesota Boy's First Battle," *Sabre and Bayonet: Stories of Heroism and Military Adventure*, ed. Theo. F. Rodenbough (New York: G.W. Dillingham Co., 1897), p. 41.

19. William White Blackford, *War Years With Jeb Stuart* (New York: Charles Scribner's Sons, 1945), p. 30.

20. CCW, p. 169.

21. Casler, p. 27.

22. William Lochren, "Narrative of the First Regiment," *Minnesota in the Civil and Indian Wars, 1861–1865*, vol. I (St. Paul: Pioneer Press Co., 1891), pp. 9–10.

23. CCW, p. 169.

24. George Baylor, *Bull Run to Bull Run; Or, Four Years in the Army of Northern Virginia* (Washington, D.C.: Zenger Publishing Co., Inc., 1900), p. 22. Baylor graduated from Dickinson College in 1860.

25. Hennessy, p. 97.

26. Beale, p. 192.

27. J.B. Caddall, "The Pulaski Guards. Company C, 4th Virginia Infantry, at the First Battle of Manassas, July 21, 1861," *Southern Historical Society Papers*, vol. 32, p. 175.

28. Lowell Reidenbaugh, *27th Virginia Infantry* (Lynchburg, Virginia: H.E. Howard, 1993), p. 166.

29. Caddall, *Southern Historical Society Papers*, vol. 32, p. 176.

30. William Gleason Bean, *The Liberty Hall Volunteers: Stonewall's College Boys* (Charlottesville: The University Press of Virginia, 1964), pp. 45–46.

31. "Documents," in *The Rebellion Record*, vol. 4., pp. 533–34. For a detailed account of Private Lewis Francis' wounds see *The Medical and Surgical History of the War of the Rebellion*, part III, vol. II, p. 154.

32. Concerning William Ott's death see Ted Barclay's, *Liberty Hall Volunteers, Letters From the Stonewall Brigade (1861–1864)*, ed. Charles W. Turner (Berryville: Rockbridge Publishing Co., 1992), p. 25. For William L. Clark, Jr.'s wound refer to Dennis E. Frye's, *2nd Virginia* (Lynchburg: H.E. Howard, 1984), p. 89. Lieutenant Doug Ramsay's death can be found in Clarence Albert Fonerden's, *A Brief History of the Military Career of Carpenter's Battery* (New Market, Virginia: Henkel and Company, 1911), p. 11.

33. "Documents," in *The Rebellion Record*, vol. 4., p. 533.

34. Walter Clark, ed., *Histories of the Several Regiments and Battalions from North Carolina in the Great War 1861–'65*, vol. I (Wendell, North Carolina: Broadfoot, 1982), pp. 297–99 and pp. 340–46; vol. V, pp. 29–33 and 581–85. See also Richard M. Iobst, *The Bloody Sixth: The Sixth North Carolina Regiment Confederate States of America* (Raleigh: Christian Printing Co., 1965), pp. 20–28.

There is some debate among the 6th North Carolina concerning who fired upon their rear ranks. Some speculate it was the 4th Alabama. Major Isaac Avery theorized it was the 11th Massachusetts, wearing gray uniforms, and mistakenly identified as Confederate troops.

35. Fonerden, p. 12. See also Robert C. Wallace, *A Few Memories of a Long Life*, ed. John M. Carroll (Fairfield, Washington: Ye Galleon Press, 1988), p. 14.

36. Fonerden, p. 13.

37. Henry N. Blake, *Three Years in the Army of the Potomac* (Boston: Lee and Shepard, 1865), p. 23.

38. J. Gray McAllister, *Sketch of Captain Thompson McAllister, Citizen, Soldier, Christian* (Petersburg: Fenn & Owen, 1896), pp. 16–17.

39. Hennessy, p. 101.

40. John N. Opie, *A Rebel Cavalryman With Lee, Stuart and Jackson* (Chicago: W.B. Conkey Co., 1899), p. 34.

41. Hutchinson, p. 24.

42. Opie, p. 32.

43. Ibid., p. 34; *CCW*, p. 244 and "Documents," *The Rebellion Record*, vol. 4, p. 533.

44. R.T. Coles, p. 23 and p. 237; In *Our Living And Our Dead: Devoted to North Carolina—Her Past, Her Present And Her Future.* (Raleigh: Southern Historical Society, September 1874 to February 1875), vol. I, p. 564, William O. Hudson, 4th Alabama, remembered Bee said, "follow me, let us support Jackson; see he stands like a stone wall." See also, Hennessy, p. 83. Tradition has always portrayed Bee stating this as his units were retreating from Matthews Hill and just as Jackson's brigade arrived. His statement, however, does not make sense at this time. As soon as Jackson arrived on Henry Hill he ordered his men to lie down and protect themselves from the Union artillery shells. They were neither standing nor fighting. For more information see Hennessy, p. 152 endnote 52.

45. Opie, p. 26.

46. *Our Living And Our Dead*, vol. I, p. 564. See also *B&L*, vol. 1, p. 237. See letter of W.A. Evans, in Maud Morrow Brown's, *The University Greys: Co. A Eleventh Mississippi Regiment Army of Northern Virginia 1861–1865* (Richmond: Garrett and Massie Inc., 1940), pp. 18–19. Evans' account differs with Hudson's in that Evans stated Bee was mortally wounded while planting the 4th Alabama's flag. W.A. Evans, however, was not at the battle and this information must have been second-hand. All first-hand accounts place Bee on his horse at the time of his wounding.

47. *Savannah Republican*, August 1, 1861.

48. Hennessy, p. 103; Sherman, pp. 183–84.

49. Brigadier General Thomas S. Allen, "The Second Wisconsin at the First Battle of Bull Run," *War Papers: Read Before the Commandery of the State of Wisconsin, Military Order of the Loyal Legion of the United States*, vol. I (Milwaukee: Burdick, Armitage and Allen, 1891), p. 389.

50. Gaff, p. 210.

51. Ibid., p. 223.

52. Ibid., p. 224.

53. George H. Otis, *The Second Wisconsin Infantry*, ed. Alan D. Gaff (Dayton, Ohio: Morningside, 1984), p. 39. Colonel Coon did not lead the 2d Wisconsin because Colonel Sherman assigned Coon to his personal staff, and put Lieutenant Colonel Peck in charge of the 2d. Sherman realized Coon was a "good hearted gentleman, who knew no more of the military art than a child; wheras...Peck, had been to West Point, and knew the drill." See Sherman's *Memoirs*, p. 180.

54. Todd, *The Seventy-Ninth Highlanders*, pp. 37–38.

55. Gaff, p. 227.

56. Hampton may have injured his ankle when his horse fell during the Young's Branch/Robinson house engagement. The first-hand accounts differ in where Hampton was wounded—ankle or head. Captain James Conner, in a letter to his mother dated July 22, 1861, stated "Hampton was shot through the leg but refused to leave the ground and fought the battle out, limping on one leg." See letter at University of South Carolina Library, Archives. Another letter by a James Griffin, Hampton's Legion, wrote his wife, on July 27, 1861, "Col. Hampton himself was slightly wounded. A ball struck him in the temple." See Civil War Times Illustrated Collection, James Griffin, Hampton Legion, 5th S.C. Reserve Inf. and 1st S.C. Militia. Transcribed letter found at the U.S. Army Military History Institute's Archives Division, Carlisle, Pennsylvania. The third letter, ironically, is written by another "James." No last name was given, and he is a different legionnaire. In a letter to his cousin dated July 26, 1861, he recalled, "The Colonel is struck by a buckshot (probably from a percussion shell) over the left eye; it has not been extracted & the doctors think it may have rebounded from a bone." Letter found in the Manassas National Battlefield Park collection. Hampton's biographer, Manly Wade Wellman, also stated Hampton suffered a slight bullet gash on his head, see Manly W. Wellman, *Giant in Gray: A Biography of Wade Hampton of South Carolina* (New York: Charles Scribner's Sons, 1949), p. 64. In the midst of battle it is quite feasible Hampton was slightly wounded in the head and ankle. We know these wounds were not life threatening, and he was not confined to a bed. Hampton in his official report did not specify the location of his wound. He stated he suffered a slight wound. See O.R., vol. II, p. 567.

57. Captain D.P. Conyngham, A.D.C., *The Irish Brigade and Its Campaigns: With Some Account of the Corcoran Legion, and Sketches of the Principal Officers* (Boston: Patrick Donahoe, 1869), p. 43.

58. Lieutenant Richard Lewis, *Camp Life of a Confederate Boy, Of Bratton's Brigade, Longstreet's Corps, C.S.A.* (Charleston: News and Courier Book Presses, 1883), pp. 13–14.

59. O.R., vol. II, p. 415.

60. Conyngham, p. 37.

61. Robert E. Withers, M.D., *Autobiography of an Octogenarian* (Roanoke: Stone Printing and MFG. Co. Press, 1907), p. 149.

Chapter 10

1. Hennessy, p. 109.

2. O.R., vol. II, p. 422.

3. George W. Bicknell, *History of the Fifth Maine Volunteers* (Portland: Hall L. Davis, 1871), pp. 30–31.

4. Jim Burgess, Director of the Museum at the Manassas National Battlefield Park, personal letter, January 19,1996.

5. Carter, p. 14.

6. Haynes, pp. 32–34.

7. Howard, p. 38.

Chapter 11

1. Brigadier General Heintzelman stated in his official report, "...we commenced our retreat about 4:30 p.m." See O.R., vol. II, p. 403.

2. Ibid.

3. Merritt, pp. 44–48.

4. Richard Moe, *The Last Full Measure: The Life and Death of the First Minnesota Volunteers* (New York: Henry Holt and Co., 1993), p. 58.

5. Rhodes, p. 34.

6. Hains, "The First Gun at Bull Run," *Cosmopolitan Magazine*, vol. 51, p. 394.

7. O.R., vol. II, p. 316.

8. Hains, p. 396.

9. Ibid., pp. 395–99.

10. J. Gray McAllister, pp. 19–20.

11. *B&L*, vol. I, p. 191.

12. "Rumors and Incidents," *The Rebellion Record*, vol. II, p. 16.

13. J. Gray McAllister, p. 26.

14. Ibid., pp. 26–27. See also Thomas D. Marbaker, *History of the Eleventh New Jersey Volunteers From Its Organization to Appomattox* (Trenton, New Jersey: MacCrelish and Quigley Printers, 1898), pp. 346–49. Two brothers which did meet after the battle were Confederate Private Frederick L. Hubbard, 3d Company, Battalion Washington Artillery, from New Orleans and Union Private Henry A. Hubbard, Company H, 1st Minnesota. Fred, age 22, found his younger brother in a field hospital. Henry, age 20, was struck by a bullet in the right shoulder, and Fred was injured by a caisson wheel which rolled over his right arm. Due to his injury Fred was discharged October 30, 1861; Henry was mustered out on December 15, 1861. See letter by "M.F." dated, July 27,1861, to the editors of the *Richmond Dispatch* found in the Manassas National Battlefield Park archives.

Chapter 12

1. Hennessy, p. 117.

2. O.R., vol. II, p. 542.

3. O.R., vol. II, p. 497. Beauregard stated, "this pursuit was soon recalled in consequence of a false report which unfortunately reached us that the enemy's reserves, known to be fresh and of considerable strength, were threatening the position of Union Mills Ford."

4. Colonel John Scott, "The Black Horse Cavalry," *The Annals of the Civil War*, ed. Gary W. Gallagher (New York: Da Capo Press, 1994), pp. 590–93; O.R., vol. II, pp. 532–35.

5. Alexander, *Fighting for the Confederacy*, p. 55.

6. Ibid.

7. Alfred Ely, *Journal of Alfred Ely, A Prisoner of War in Richmond*, ed. Charles Lanman (New York: D. Appleton and Company, 1862), pp. 15–16. See also Hennessy, pp. 119–20.

Chapter 13

1. Iobst, p. 24. It should be noted that many of the survivors drank from these very streams and became very ill. Colonel Withers of the 28th Virginia recalled nearly half of "our men were in the Hospitals and many died," see Withers, p. 152.

2. Opie, p. 40.

3. Howard, pp. 41–42.

4. Casler, pp. 29–30.

5. R.M. Johnston, *Bull Run: Its Strategy and Tactics*, p. 255.

6. O.R., vol. II, p. 477.

Chapter 14

1. Carl Sandburg, *Abraham Lincoln: The War Years*, vol. I (New York: Harcourt, Brace and Company, 1939), pp. 302–3.

Chapter 15

1. OR., vol. II, p. 758.
2. T. Harry Williams, *Lincoln and His Generals* (New York: Vintage Books, 1952), pp. 24–25.
3. Todd, *American Military Equipage 1851–1872*, "The United States Army," part I, vol. I, p. 45.
4. Williams, *P.G.T. Beauregard*, p. 107. For a full account of Beauregard's and Davis's feud see pp. 96–112.
5. Stephen W. Sears, *To the Gates of Richmond: The Peninsula Campaign* (New York: Ticknor & Fields, 1992), pp. 138–40.

Epilogue

1. O.R., vol. II, p. 987.
2. Zettler, pp. 70–71.
3. Sherman, pp. 188–89.
4. Ibid., pp. 190–91.
5. Fairchild, p. 19.
6. Allan Nevins, *The War for the Union*, vol. I (New York: Charles Scribner's Sons, 1959), p. 221.
7. *The Rebellion Record*, vol. II., pp. 110–11.
8. Ibid., p. 110.
9. Ibid., p. 113.

Appendix I

1. O.R., vol. II, pp. 503, 571.

PHOTOGRAPHS—BIBLIOGRAPHY

(In order of appearance)

Abbreviations:

Miller: Francis T. Miller, *The Photographic History of The Civil War.* 10 vols. New York: The Review of Reviews Co., 1912.

MNP: Manassas National Park. Museum Director, Jim Burgess.

USAMHI: United States Army Military History Institute. Photo archivists, Mike Winey and Randy Hackenburg.

A drawing of a mother weeping, Prof. J. Warren Gilbert's, *The Blue and Gray: A History of the Conflicts During Lee's Invasion And Battle of Gettysburg.* 1922.

Brig. Gen. P.G.T. Beauregard, USAMHI.

Gen. Joseph Johnston, USAMHI.

Brig. Gen. Irvin McDowell, USAMHI.

Brig. Gen. Milledge Bonham, USAMHI.

Brig. Gen. Richard Ewell, USAMHI.

Brig. Gen. James Longstreet, USAMHI.

Col. Philip St. George Cocke, Miller, vol. 10.

Col. Jubal Early, USAMHI.

Col. Nathan Evans, USAMHI.

Brig. Gen. Theophilus Holmes, Miller, vol. 10.

Col. Wade Hampton, USAMHI.

Brig. Gen. Thomas Jackson, USAMHI.

Col. Francis Bartow, USAMHI.

Brig. Gen. Barnard Bee, USAMHI.

Col. Arnold Elzey, USAMHI.

Col. James Stuart, USAMHI.

Brig. Gen. Daniel Tyler, USAMHI.

Col. David Hunter, USAMHI.

Col. Samuel Heintzelman, USAMHI.

Col. Dixon Miles, USAMHI.

Maj. Gen. Robert Patterson, USAMHI.

Lt. Gen. Winfield Scott, USAMHI.

Maj. Sullivan Ballou, Wiley Sword Coll. via USAMHI.

Pvt. Martin Haynes, *A History of the Second Regiment, New Hampshire Volunteer Infantry*, 1896.

Col. Israel Richardson, USAMHI.

Lt. William H.B. Smith, USAMHI.

Orderly Sgt. William H. Morgan, *Personal Reminiscences of the War of 1861–1865*. Lynchburg: J.P. Bell Co., Inc., 1911.

Wilmer McLean, Appomattox Court House National Park.

Maj. John Barnard, USAMHI.

Gov. William Sprague, *The History of Battery A, First Rhode Island Light Artillery in the War to Preserve the Union 1861–1865*. 1904.

Col. William T. Sherman, USAMHI.

Brig. Gen. Robert Schenck, USAMHI.

Lt. Peter Hains, *Cosmopolitan Magazine*, vol. 51 (1911).

30-pounder Parrott, USAMHI.

Capt. Edward P. Alexander, USAMHI.

Chaplain Augustus Woodbury, USAMHI.

Pvt. Elisha H. Rhodes, USAMHI.

Lt. Col. Francis S. Fiske, *History of the Second Regiment, New Hampshire...*, 1896.

Matthews House, USAMHI.

Stone House, USAMHI.

Col. Ambrose Burnside, Klinepeter Coll. via USAMHI.

Pvt. Thomas Aldrich, *The History of Battery A...*, 1904.

Lt. William Weeden, *The History of Battery A...*, 1904.

Maj. C.R. Wheat, *Confederate Veteran*, vol. 19.

Capt. William Reynolds, *The History of Battery A...*, 1904.

Col. John S. Slocum, USAMHI.

Lt. Col. Frank Wheaton, USAMHI.

Maj. Joseph P. Balch, USAMHI.

Col. Andrew Porter, USAMHI.

Col. Egbert Jones, Alabama Department of Archives and History, Montgomery, Alabama.

Lt. Col. Evander Law, USAMHI.

Capt. Lewis E. Lindsay, Quinn Coll. via USAMHI.

Lt. James H. Young, White-Thomas Coll. via USAMHI.

Dr. Watkins Vaughan, taken from *Reuben Vaughan Kidd: Soldier of the Confederacy*. Petersburg: Violent Bank, 1947.

James Jefferson, *Reuben Vaughan Kidd*

Lt. Col. William M. Gardner, Miller, vol. 10.

Col. Gilman Marston, USAMHI.

Col. Henry P. Martin, USAMHI.

Maj. George Sykes, USAMHI.

Lt. Eugene Carter,

Col. Henry W. Slocum, *History of the 27th Regiment N.Y. Vols.*, 1888.

Col. Lucius Gartrell, Miller, vol. 10.

Pvt. John Coxe, *Confederate Veteran*, vol. 23 (1915).

Adj. Theodore Barker, Dr. Gaillard Waterfall Coll. via South Carolina Confederate Relic Room and Museum, Columbia, South Carolina.

Adj. John Jenkins, Gladstone Coll. via USAMHI.

Capt. William Averell, USAMHI.

Lt. Harry T. Buford and Madame Loreta Janeta Velazquez, *The Woman in Battle*, 1876.

Capt. John Imboden, USAMHI.

Robinson's House, USAMHI.

Sudley Road, USAMHI.

Capt. Romeyn B. Ayres, USAMHI.

Capt. James Haggerty, USAMHI.

Pvt. John Opie, *A Rebel Cavalryman with Lee, Stuart and Jackson*, 1899.

Col. Charles D. Jameson, USAMHI.

Col. John L. Chatfield, USAMHI.

Col. Wade Hampton, USAMHI.

Col. Erasmus Keyes, USAMHI.

A drawing of Robinson's House, *Battles and Leaders*, 1894.

Color Sgt. William S. Deane, James Mundy via USAMHI.

Capt. Elisha N. Jones, James Mundy via USAMHI.

Maj. William Barry, USAMHI.

Capt. Charles Griffin, USAMHI.

Capt. James B. Ricketts, USAMHI.

Lt. Charles Hazlett, USAMHI.

Drawing of Mrs. Henry's house by Fremaux, Nelson Coll. via USAMHI.

Pvt. John Casler, *Four Years in the Stonewall Brigade*, 1906.

Col. William Gorman, USAMHI.

Col. Noah Farnham, USAMHI.

Sgt. John G. Merritt, USAMHI.

Lt. William Blackford, taken from *War Years With Jeb Stuart*. New York: Charles Scribner's Sons, 1945.

Capt. William Colvill, Jr., USAMHI.

Col. Alfred M. Wood, USAMHI.

Pvt. George Baylor, May Morris Room, Dickinson College Library.

Pvt. William Ott, MNP.

Lt. Col. John Echols, USAMHI.

Lt. Col. E.B. Fowler, USAMHI.

Col. William Smith, USAMHI.

Col. Orlando Willcox, USAMHI.

Col. Charles Fisher, *Histories of the Several Regiments and Battalions from North Carolina in the Great War 1861–1865*, 1901.

Pvt. Lewis Francis, *The Medical and Surgical History of the War of the Rebellion*, part 3, vol. II, 1883, page 154.

Sgt. James C. McKelsey, MNP.

Capt. William L. Clark, Jr., Herren Coll. via USAMHI.

Lt. Charles Norris, MNP.

Lt. Doug Ramsay, Borrell Sr. Coll. via USAMHI.

Pvt. Augustus Brown, USAMHI.

Capt. Isaac Avery, *Histories of the Several Regiments and Battalions from North Carolina in the Great War 1861–1865*, vol. I, 1901.

Lt. Willie Mangum, ibid.

Pvt. James W. Crowell, Crowell Coll. via USAMHI.

Col. Samuel Lawrence, USAMHI.

Col. George Clark, Jr., USAMHI.

Sgt. Henry Blake, USAMHI.

Capt. Thompson McAllister, *Sketch of Captain Thompson McAllister, Citizen, Soldier, Christian,* 1896.

A drawing of Ricketts and Harman shaking hands on the battlefield, *A Rebel Cavalryman...,* 1899.

Pvt. William Woodward, *A Rebel Cavalryman...,* 1899.

Col. Isaac F. Quinby, Hunt Coll. via USAMHI.

Maj. James Wadsworth, USAMHI.

Cpl. Willie Upham, *Racine County Militant* (1915) via Racine Heritage Museum, Racine, Wisconsin.

Capt. Andrew J. Langworthy, Milwaukee Historical Society.

Capt. John Mansfield, Library of Congress, LCB812-9082.

Col. James Cameron, USAMHI.

A drawing of Colonel Cameron's death, *The Seventy-Ninth Highlanders,* 1886.

Capt. James Conner, Millers, vol. 10.

Col. Michael Corcoran, Colling Coll. via USAMHI.

Col. Hobart Ward, USAMHI.

Col. Eppa Hunton, USAMHI.

Col. Joseph Kershaw, USAMHI.

Capt. Thomas Meagher, USAMHI.

Col. Oliver O. Howard, USAMHI.

Col. Joseph B. Kershaw, USAMHI.

Col Hiram C. Berry, USAMHI.

Col. E.B.C. Cash, South Caroliniana Library, University of South Carolina, Columbia, South Carolina.

Col. Henry Whiting, USAMHI.

Pvt. George Bicknell, USAMHI.

Orderly Sgt. McHenry Howard, *Recollections of a Maryland Confederate Soldier and Staff Officer,* 1914.

Capt. S. James Smith, Gladstone Coll. via USAMHI.

Lt. Edmund Kirby, USAMHI.

Lt. Peter Hains, *Cosmopolitan Magazine,* vol. 51, 1911.

Capt. Thompson McAllister, "Sketch of Captain Thompson McAllister, 1896."

Lt. Col. Robert McAllister, USAMHI.

Col. Micah Jenkins, Millers, vol. 10.

Pvt. Thomas Fowler, Union County Musuem via South Carolina
    Confederate Relic Room and Museum.

Lt. Col. Thomas Munford, USAMHI.

A drawing of a Black Horse cavalryman by Fremaux, Nelson Coll.
    via USAMHI.

Alfred Ely, *Journal of Alfred Ely, A Prisoner of War in Richmond*,
    1862.

Brig. Gen. McDowell and Maj. Gen. McClellan, USAMHI.

BIBLIOGRAPHY

Aldrich, Thomas M. *The History of Battery A, First Rhode Island Light Artillery in the War to Preserve the Union 1861–1865*. Providence: Snow and Farnham, 1904.

Alexander, Edward P. *Fighting for the Confederacy: The Personal Recollections of General Edward Porter Alexander*. Ed. Gary W. Gallagher, Chapel Hill: The University of North Carolina Press, 1989.

———. "The Battle of Bull Run." *Scribners Magazine*. Vol. XLI (1907), pp. 80–94.

Allen, Thomas S. "The Second Wisconsin at the First Battle of Bull Run." *War Papers Read Before the Commandery of the State of Wisconsin, Military Order of the Loyal Legion of the United States*. Vol. I. Milwaukee: Burdick, Amitage & Allen, 1891.

Averell, William W. *Ten Years in the Saddle: The Memoirs of William Woods Averell*. Eds. Edward K. Eckert and Nicholas J. Amato, San Rafael: Presidio Press, 1978.

Barclay, Ted. *Liberty Hall Volunteers Letters from the Stonewall Brigade (1861–1864)*. Ed. Charles W. Turner, Berryville: Rockbridge Publishing Co., 1992.

Basler, Roy P., ed. *The Collected Works of Abraham Lincoln*. Vol. IV. New Brunswick: Rutgers University Press, 1953.

Baylor, George. *Bull Run to Bull Run; Or, Four Years in the Army of Northern Virginia*. Washington, D.C.: Zenger Publishing Co., Inc., 1900.

Beale, R.L.T. *History of the Ninth Virginia Cavalry, In the War Between the States*. Richmond: B.F. Johnson Publishing Co., 1899.

Bean, William G. *The Liberty Hall Volunteers: Stonewall's College Boys*. Charlottesville: The University Press of Virginia, 1964.

Beauregard, P.G.T. *A Commentary on the Campaign and Battle of Manassas of July 1861 Together With a Summary of the Art of War*. New York: Putnams, 1891.

———. "The First Battle of Bull Run." *Battles and Leaders Of the Civil War*. Vol. I, pp. 196–227.

Bicknell, George W. *History of the Fifth Maine Volunteers*. Portland: Hall L. Davis, 1871.

Blackford, William W. *War Years With Jeb Stuart*. New York: Charles Scribner's Sons, 1945.

Blake, Henry N. *Three Years In the Army of the Potomac*. Boston: Lee and Shepard, 1865.

Boatner, Mark M. *The Civil War Dictionary*. New York: Vintage Books, 1991.

Caddall, J.B. "The Pulaski Guards. Company C, 4th Virginia Infantry, at the First Battle of Manassas, July 21, 1861." *Southern Historical Society Papers*. Vol. 32, pp. 174–78.

Carter, Captain Robert G. *Four Brothers In Blue Or Sunshine and Shadows of the War of the Rebellion: A Story of the Great Civil War from Bull Run to Appomattox*. Austin: University of Texas Press, 1913.

Casler, John O. *Four Years in the Stonewall Brigade*. Girard, Kansas: Appeal Publishing Co., 1906.

Chestney, T.O. "Blucher of the Day at Manassas." *Confederate Veteran*. Vol. 7, p. 310.

Clark, Walter, ed. *Histories of the Several Regiments and Battalions from North Carolina in the Great War 1861–1865*. 5 vols. Goldsboro, North Carolina: Nash Brothers, Book and Job Printers, 1901.

Coggins, Jack. *Arms and Equipment of the Civil War*. Garden City: Doubleday and Company Inc., 1962.

Coles, R.T. *From Huntsville to Appomattox: R.T. Coles's History of 4th Regiment, Alabama Volunteer Infantry, C.S.A. Army of Northern Virginia*. Ed. Jeffrey D. Stocker, Knoxville: The University of Tennessee Press, 1996.

Comings, Harrison H. *Personal Reminiscences of Company E, New York Fire Zouaves, Better Known As Ellsworth's Fire Zouaves*. Malden, Massachusetts: J. Gould Tilden, Steam Book, 1886. Found at U.S. Military History Institute, Archives Division, Carlisle, Pennsylvania.

Conrad, D.B. "History of the First Battle of Manassas and the Organization of the Stonewall Brigade." *Southern Historical Society Papers*. Vol. 19, pp. 88–94.

Conyngham, D.P. *The Irish Brigade and Its Campaigns: With Some Account of the Corcoran Legion, and Sketches of the Principal Officers*. Boston: Patrick Donahoe, 1869.

Coxe, John. "The Battle of First Manassas." *Confederate Veteran.* Vol. 23, pp. 24–26.

Crute, Joseph H., Jr. *Emblems of Southern Valor: The Battle Flags of the Confederacy.* Louisville: Harmony House, 1990.

Cudworth, Warren H. *History of the First Regiment (Massachusetts Infantry).* Boston: Walker, Fuller, and Co., 1866.

Cummings, Arthur C. "Thirty-third Virginia at Manassas." *Southern Historical Society Papers.* Vol. 34, pp. 363–71.

Cunningham, Horace H. *Field Medical Services at the Battles of Manassas (Bull Run).* Athens, Georgia: University of Georgia Press, 1968.

Davis, Jefferson, Jr. *The Rise and Fall of the Confederate Government.* 2 vols. New York: D. Appleton and Co., 1881.

Davis, William C. *Battle at Bull Run: A History of the First Major Campaign of the Civil War.* Garden City, New York: Doubleday and Company Inc., 1977.

———. *First Blood: Fort Sumter to Bull Run.* Alexandria: Time-Life Books, 1983.

de Trobriand, Regis. *Four Years With The Army of the Potomac.* Trans. George K. Dauchy. Boston: Ticknor and Company, 1889.

de Vattel, M. *The Law of Nations or Principles of the Law of Nature.* Trans. Joseph Chitty. Samuel Campbell, 1796.

Dufour, Charles L. *Gentle Tiger: The Gallant Life of Roberdeau Wheat.* Baton Rouge: Louisiana State University Press, 1957.

Dupuy, Trevor N. et al. *Dictionary of Military Terms: A Guide to the Language of Warfare and Military Institutions.* New York: H.W. Wilson Company, 1986.

Ely, Alfred. *Journal of Alfred Ely, A Prisoner of War in Richmond.* Ed. Charles Lanman, New York: D. Appleton and Company, 1862.

Fairchild, Charles B. *History of the 27th Regiment N.Y. Vols.* Binghamton: Carl and Matthews, 1888.

Finch, George M. "Boys of '61." *G.A.R. Papers.* Vol. I. Cincinnati: Fred C. Jones Post, 1891.

Fiske, Francis S. "Second New Hampshire Regiment at Bull Run." N.p. n.d. Found at the U.S. Military History Institute, Reference Section, Carlisle, Pennsylvania.

First Manassas (Bull Run) And the War Around It.... Manasass: First Manassas Corp., 1961.

Fonerden, C.A. *A Brief History of the Military Career of Carpenter's Battery.* New Market: Henkel and Co., 1911.

Freeman, Douglas S. *Lee's Lieutenants: A Study in Command.* 3 Vols. New York: Charles Scribner's Sons, 1942.

Fry, James B. "McDowell's Advance To Bull Run." *Battles and Leaders of the Civil War,* Vol. I, pp. 167–93.

———. *McDowell and Tyler in the Campaign of Bull Run, 1861.* New York: Van Nostrand, 1884.

Frye, Dennis E. *2nd Virginia Infantry.* Lynchburg, Virginia: H.E. Howard, 1984.

Fuller, J.F.C. *Alexander the Great.* New York: Da Capo Press, 1960.

Gaff, Alan D. *If this is War: A History of the Campaign of Bull's Run by the Wisconsin Regiment Thereafter Known as the Ragged Ass Second.* Dayton: Morningside, 1991.

Goldsborough, W.W. *The Maryland Line in the Confederate Army 1861–1865.* Baltimore, Maryland: Guggenheimer, Weil and Co., 1900.

Hains, General Peter C. "The First Gun at Bull Run." *Cosmopolitan Magazine.* Vol. 51 (1911), pp. 388–400.

Hanson, Joseph M. *Bull Run Remembers...The History, Traditions and Landmarks of the Manassas (Bull Run) Campaigns Before Washington 1861–1862.* Manassas: National Capitol Publisher Inc., 1953.

Hardee, William J. *Rifle and Light Infantry Tactics.* 2 Vols. Philadelphia: Lippencot, Grambo & Co., 1855 and 1861.

Harrison, George F. "Ewell at First Manassas." *Southern Historical Society Papers.* Vol. 14 (1886), pp. 355–57.

Haynes, Martin. *A History of the Second Regiment, New Hampshire Volunteer Infantry.* Lakeport, New Hampshire, 1896.

Henderson, G.F.R. *Stonewall Jackson and the American Civil War.* 2 Vols. Secaucus, New Jersey: Blue and Grey.

Henderson, Lindsey P. *The Oglethorpe Light Infantry.* Savannah and Chatham County: The Civil War Centennial Commission, 1961.

Hennessy, John. *The First Battle of Manassas: An End To Innocence July 18–21.* Lynchburg, Virginia: H.E. Howard, Inc., 1989.

———. "The First Hour's Fight On Henry Hill." Manassas National Park Archives, 1985.

Holcombe, Return I. *History of the First Regiment Minnesota Volunteer Infantry: 1861–1865.* Minnesota: Easto and Masterman, 1916.

Howard, McHenry. *Recollections of a Maryland Confederate Soldier and Staff Officer.* Baltimore: Williams and Wilkens Co., 1914.

Hundley, George A. "Beginning and the Ending." *Southern Historical Society Papers.* Vol. 23, 1896.

Hutchinson, Gustavus B. *A Narrative of the Formation and Services of the Eleventh Massachusetts Volunteers, From April 15, 1861, to July 14, 1865.* Boston: Alfred Mudge and Son, 1893.

Imboden, John D. "Incidents of the First Bull Run." *Battles and Leaders.* Vol. I. Eds. Robert U. Johnson and Clarence C. Buel. New York: Castle, 1888.

Imholte, John Q. *The First Volunteers: History of the First Minnesota Volunteer Regiment 1861–1865.* Minneapolis: Ross and Haines, 1963.

Iobst, Richard W. *The Bloody Sixth: The Sixth North Carolina Regiment Confederate States of America.* Raleigh: Christian Printing Co., 1965.

Irby, Richard. *Historical Sketch of the Nottoway Grays.* Richmond: J.W. Fergusson & Son, 1878.

Johnston, David E. *Four Years A Soldier.* Princeton, West Virginia, 1887.

Johnston, Joseph E. "Responsibilities of the First Bull Run." *Battles and Leaders.* Eds. Robert U. Johnson and Clarence C. Buel. New York: Castle, 1888.

Johnston, Robert M. *Bull Run: Its Strategy and Tactics.* New York: Houghton Mifflin Co., 1913.

Jones, Terry L. *Lee's Tigers: The Louisiana Infantry in the Army of Northern Virginia.* Baton Rouge: Louisiana State University Press, 1952.

Journal of Alfred Ely, A Prisoner of War in Richmond. Charles Lanman, ed. New York: D. Appleton and Company, 1862.

Journal Of The Congress Of The Confederate States Of America, 1861–1865. Vol. I. Washington, D.C.: Government Printing Office, 1904.

King, Josias R. "The Battle of Bull Run, A Confederate Victory Obtained but not Achieved" (MOLLUS, Minnesota). Minneapolis: Aug. Davis, 1909.

Lewis, Richard. *Camp Life of a Confederate Boy, Of Bratton's Brigade, Longstreet's Corps. C.S.A.* Charleston: News and Courier Book Presses, 1883.

Livermore, Thomas L. *Numbers and Losses in the Civil War in America 1861–1865.* Boston: Houghton Mifflin, 1902.

Lochren, William. "Narrative of the First Regiment." *Minnesota in the Civil War and Indian Wars 1861–1865*. Vol. I. St. Paul: Pioneer Press Co., 1891.

Longstreet, James. *From Manassas to Appomattox: Memoirs of the Civil War in America*. New York: Mallard Press, 1991.

McAfee, Michael J. *Zouaves: The First and the Bravest*. Gettysburg: Thomas Publications, 1991.

McAllister, J. Gray. *Sketch of Captain Thompson McAllister, Citizen, Soldier, Christian*. Petersburg: Fenn and Owen, 1896.

McWhiney, Grady and Perry D. Jamieson. *Attack and Die: Civil War Military Tactics and Southern Heritage*. Tuscaloosa: The University of Alabama Press, 1982.

Meagher, Thomas F. *The Last Days of the 69th in Virginia*. New York, 1861.

Merritt, John G. "A Minnesota Boy's First Battle." *Sabre and Bayonet: Stories of Heroism and Military Adventure*. Ed. Theo. F. Rodenbough. New York: G.W. Dillingham Co., 1897.

Metcalf, Lewis H. "So Eager Were We All..." *American Heritage*. Vol. XVI, Number 4, June 1965.

Middleton, Lee. *Hearts of Fire...Soldier Women of the Civil War*. Franklin: Genealogy Publishing Service, 1993.

Miller, Francis T. *The Photographic History of The Civil War*. 10 vols. New York: The Review of Reviews Co., 1912.

Moe, Richard. *The Last Full Measure: The Life and Death of the First Minnesota Volunteers*. New York: Henry Holt and Co., 1993.

Moore, Frank, ed. *The Rebellion Record: A Diary of American Events*. 10 vols. New York: G.P. Putnam, 1861.

Morgan, William H. *Personal Reminiscences of the War of 1861–1865*. Lynchburg, Virginia: J.P. Bell Co., Inc., 1911.

Morrill, Lily Logan. *My Confederate Girlhood: The Memoirs of Kate Virginia Cox Logan*. Richmond: Garrett and Massie, Inc., 1932.

Mundy, James H. *Second to None: The Story of the 2nd Maine Volunteers "The Bangor Regiment."* Scarborough: Harp Publications, 1992.

Murphy, Terrence V. *10th Virginia Infantry*. Lynchburg: H.E. Howard, Inc., 1989.

Naisawald, L. Van Loan. *Grape and Canister: The Story of the Field Artillery of the Army of the Potomac, 1861–1865*. New York: Oxford University Press, 1960.

Nevins, Allan. *The War for the Union.* Vol. I. New York: Charles Scribner's Sons, 1959.

Opie, John N. *A Rebel Cavalryman With Lee, Stuart and Jackson.* Chicago: W.B. Conkey Co., 1899.

Otis, George A. and D.L. Huntington. *The Medical and Surgical History of the War of the Rebellion.* Part 3, vol. II. Washington: Government Printing Office, 1883.

Otis, George H. *The Second Wisconsin Infantry.* Ed. Alan Gaff. Dayton: Morningside, 1984.

Our Firemen. Chapter XLII, "Fire Zouaves." U.S. Military History Institute, Archives Division, Carlisle, Pennsylvania.

Our Living and Our Dead: Devoted to North Carolina—Her Past, Her Present and Her Future. Vol. I. Raleigh: Southern Historical Society, September 1874 to February.

Owen, William M. *In Camp and Battle with the Washington Artillery of New Orleans.* Boston: Ticknor and Company, 1885.

Parker, Dangerfield. "Personal Reminiscences: The Regular Infantry at Bull Run." *United States Service.* XII, 1885.

Paxton, Elisha F. *The Civil War Letters of General Frank "Bull" Paxton, CSA. A Lieutenant of Lee & Jackson.* John G. Paxton, ed. Hillsboro: Hill Jr. College Press, 1978.

Peters, Winfield. "First Battle of Manassas." *Southern Historical Society Papers.* Vol. 34, 1906.

Peterson, Harold L. *Round Shot and Rammers.* New York: Bonanza Books, 1969.

Pierrepont, Alice V.D. *Reuben Vaughan Kidd: Soldier of the Confederacy.* Petersburg: Violent Bank, 1947.

Preble, George H. *History of the Flag of the United States of America.* Boston: James R. Osgood and Company, 1882.

Reese, Timothy. *Sykes' Regular Infantry Division, 1861–1865.* Jefferson: McFarland & Co., Inc., 1990.

Reid, Jesse W. *History of the Fourth Regiment S.C. Volunteers.* Greenville: Shannon & Co., 1892.

Rhodes, Elisha Hunt. *All For the Union: The Civil War Diary and Letters of Elisha Hunt Rhodes.* Ed. Robert Hunt Rhodes. New York: Orion Books, 1985.

Robertson, Dr. James I. *The 4th Virginia Infantry.* Lynchburg: H.E. Howard, 1982.

———. *The Stonewall Brigade.* Baton Rouge: Louisiana State University Press, 1963.

Robinson, Frank T. *History of the Fifth Regiment, M.V.M.* Boston: W.F. Brown and Co., 1879.

Roe, Alfred S. *The Fifth Regiment Massachusetts Volunteer Infantry.* Boston: Fifth Regiment Veteran Association, 1911.

Ropes, John C. *The Story of the Civil War.* Part I. New York: G.P. Putnam's Sons, 1933.

Sandburg, Carl. *Abraham Lincoln: The War Years.* 7 vols. New York: Harcourt, Brace and Company, 1939.

Scott, John. "The Black Horse Cavalry." *The Annals of the Civil War.* Ed. Gary W. Gallagher. New York: Da Capo Press, 1994.

Sherman, William T. *Memoirs of General William T. Sherman.* New York: Da Capo Press, 1984.

Smith, William. "Reminiscences of the First Battle of Manassas." *Southern Historical Society Papers.* Vol. 10. 1882.

The Soldier in the Civil War: A Pictorial History of the Conflict, 1861–1865. New York: J.H. Brown Pub. Co., 1884.

Sorrel, Gilbert Moxley. *Recollections of a Confederate Staff Officer.* New York: The Neale Publishing Co., 1905.

Starbuck, Gregory J. "Up Alabamians!" *Military Images.* July–August 1986.

Telfer, William D. *A Reminiscence of the First Battle of Manassas: A Camp-fire Story of the Seventy-first Regiment, N.G.S.N.Y.* Brooklyn: W.D. Telfer, 1864.

Tevis, C. *The History of the Fighting Fourteenth.* Baltimore: Butternut and Blue, 1993.

Todd, Frederick. *American Military Equipage 1851–1872.* 3 vols. Providence: The Company of Military Historians, 1974.

———. *American Military Equipage 1851–1872.* Ser. II, "State Forces." Chatham Square Press, Inc., 1983.

Todd, William. *The Seventy-Ninth Highlanders.* Albany: Brandow, Barton and Co., 1886.

U.S. Congress. *Report of the Joint Committee on the Conduct of the War, In Three Parts: Bull Run to Ball's Bluff.* Part II. Washington, D.C.: Government Printing Office, 1863.

Velazquez, Madame Loreta Janeta. *The Woman in Battle: A Narrative of the Exploits, Adventures and Travels of Madame Loreta Janeta Velazquez, Otherwise Known As Lieutenant Harry T. Buford.* Ed. C.J. Worthington. Hartford: T. Belknap, 1876.

Wallace, Lee, Jr., *5th Virginia Infantry.* Lynchburg, Virginia: H.E. Howard, 1988.

Wallace, Robert C. *A Few Memories of a Long Life.* Ed. John M. Carroll. Fairfield, Washington: Ye Galleon Press, 1988.

The War of the Rebellion: A Compilation of the Official Records of the Union and Confederate Armies. Ser. I. Vol. II and vol. LI, pt. I. Washington, D.C.: Government Printing Office, 1880–1901.

Warder, T.B. & Jas. M. Catlett. *Battle of Young's Branch or Manassas Plain.* Richmond: Enquirer Book and Job Press, 1862.

Warner, Ezra. *Generals in Gray.* Baton Rouge: Louisiana State University Press, 1959.

———. *Generals in Blue.* Baton Rouge: Louisiana State University Press, 1964.

Wellman, Manly W. *Giant in Gray: A Biography of Wade Hampton of South Carolina.* New York: Charles Scribner's Sons, 1949.

Wiley, Bell Irvin. *The Life of Billy Yank: The Common Soldier of the Union.* Baton Rouge: Louisiana State University Press, 1981.

———. *The Life of Johnny Reb: The Common Soldier of the Confederacy.* New York: Bobbs-Merrill Co., 1943.

Williams, T. Harry. *Lincoln and His Generals.* New York: Vintage Books, 1952.

———. *P.G.T. Beauregard: Napoleon in Gray.* Baton Rouge: Louisiana State University Press, 1955.

Withers, Robert E. *Autobiography of an Octogenarian.* Roanoke: Stone Printing and MFG. Co. Press, 1907.

Woodbury, Augustus. *A Narrative of the Campaign of the First Rhode Island Regiment, in the Spring and Summer of 1861.* Providence: Sidney S. Rider, 1862.

———. *The Second Rhode Island Regiment: A Narrative of Military Operations.* Providence, 1873.

Zettler, Berrien M. *War Stories and School-Day Incidents: For the Children.* New York: Neale Publishing Co., 1912.

INDEX

References to photographs are in italics.
First names are listed where known.

Buck Hill, 78

Buford, Lt. Harry: vignette. *See also* Madame Loreta Janeta Velazquez, 82, *82*

Bull Run Creek, xii, 19, 28, 37, 41, 43, 48, 87, 91, 159, 162, 168

Burnside, Col. Ambrose E., 46, 48–51, *51*, 52–55, *57*, 60, *65*, 67, *71*, 177; asks for the U.S. Regulars, 72

C

Caddall, Pvt. J.B., 4th Va.: account of battle, 113

Cameron, Col. James, 79th N.Y., *139*; leads regiment onto Henry Hill and killed, 140

Carlisle, Capt. J.H.: unlimbers near the Stone Bridge, 41

Carter, Lt. Eugene, U.S. Regulars: description of Matthews Hill battle, 72, *72*, 156

Cash, Col. Ellerbe Boggan Crawford, 8th S.C., *151*; threatens to killed Congressman Ely, 172–73

Casler, Pvt. John, 33d Va., *102*, *105*; describes charge on Griffin's two guns, 107, *109*; finds his best friend, 174–75, *175*. *See* 203 n. 14

Catahoula Guerillas, Wheat's battalion: fight on Matthews Hill, 51–52, 58

Centreville, Va., 26, 40, 42, 154, 159, 161, 162

Charleston, S.C., ix

Chatfield, Col. John L., 3d Conn., *90*

Chinn farm, battle on, 150–58

Clark, Col. George, 11th Mass., *123*, *126*

Clark, Capt. William, 2d Va., *116*; wounded, 115

Cocke, Philip St. George, *12*; biography, 12

Colvill, Capt. William, 1st Minn., *107*; account of the battle, 107

Connecticut Troops
3d: on Henry Hill, 90–92

Conner, Capt. James, Hampton's Legion: assumes command, 140, *143*, *146*, 148. *See* 206 n. 56

Coon, Col., 2d Wis. *See* 205 n. 53

Corcoran, Col. Michael, 69th N.Y., *143*, *146*, 148; captured, 184

Coxe, Pvt. John, Hampton's Legion, *77*; describes battle near Young's Branch, 77

Crowell, Pvt. James, 4th Va., *123*; killed, 124

Cub Run, 35, 40–42, 159, 167–69

Cummings, Col. Arthur, 33d Va., 99; orders the regiment not to fire, 105; orders regiment to charge, 107

Cunningham, Pvt. Billy, 1st Mich.: killed, 119

D

Davis, Jefferson, 8, 17–18, 37, 64, 179–80

Deane, Color Sgt. William S., 2d Maine, *94*; killed, 92;

Dogan's farm, 77, 80, 97

E

Early, Col. Jubal A., *12*, *158*; biography, 12; at Blackburn's Ford, 28–29; arrives at Chinn farm, 158

Echols, Lt. Col. John, 27th Va., *111*, *119*, 123

Ely, Alfred, *172*, 172–73

Elzey, Col. Arnold, *14*; biography, 14; fights near Chinn farm, *151*, 152–53, 155, 157, *158*

Evans, Col. Nathan, *12*, 37, *39*, 43–45, 50, *51*, *57*, 60, 60–61, *65*, *71*, 74; biography, 12

Ewell, Brig. Gen. Richard, *11*, 37–38, 74; biography, 11

F

Fairchild, Cpl. Charles B., 27th N.Y., 76, 78

Fairfax Court House, Va., 17

Farnham, Col. Noah, 11th N.Y.: mortally wounded, 101, *102*

Finch, Capt. George, 2d Ohio: describes the skirmish line near the Stone Bridge, 40; describes Colonel Sherman, 43–44

Fisher, Col. Charles, 6th N.C., *112*; leads regiment onto Henry Hill and killed, 117

Fiske, Lt. Col. Francis, 2d N.H.: describes the morning of the battle, 47–48, *48*, *67*, 67, 69

Merritt, Sgt. John, 1st Minn.: account
of Henry Hill battle, 101, *102*; during
the retreat, 159
Michigan Troops
 1st: fights on Henry Hill, 117–19,
 120–21
 2d: at Blackburn's Ford, Map 5 and
 6, 29
 3d: at Blackburn's Ford, Map 5 and
 6, 29
Miles, Col. Dixon S., *16*, 161, 176;
biography, 16
Minnesota Troops
 1st, 99–101, 104–7
Mississippi Troops
 2d: battle on Matthews Hill, 65–68
 11th: on Matthews Hill, 65–68
 17th: charges across McLean's Ford,
 167
 18th: fights near McLean's Ford, 167
Mitchell's Ford, 26–27
Morgan, Ord. Sgt. William, 11th Va.:
describes the skirmish at Blackburn's
Ford, 28, *30*
Munford, Lt. Col. Thomas: leads
cavalrymen against Union soldiers
during the retreat, 162, 170, *171*
Musket. *See* Weapons

N

New Hampshire Troops
 2d: uniform of, 3; enters battle on
 Matthews Hill, 67–69; fights near
 Sudley Road, 156
New York Troops
 8th: ordered to charge, 80
 11th (Fire Zouaves), 105, 107, 130,
 144; uniform of, 3; fights on Henry
 Hill, 99–101; repulses Confederate
 cavalry attack, 103
 12th: battles near Blackburn's Ford,
 28–29
 13th: on Henry Hill, 132–33, 135
 14th Brooklyn "Red Legged Devils,"
 109, 110, 113, 117, 121, 130, 144;
 uniform of, 3; charges Henry Hill,
 Map 28, 108
 27th: fights near Young's Branch,
 77–81
 38th, 144; enters the battle on
 Henry Hill, 106

 69th: "Irish" fires into 2d Wisconsin,
 135; charges up Henry Hill, 144–48
 71st: on Matthews Hill, 67–69
 79th: "Highlanders" march to
 Manassas, 23–24; given nickname
 by Sherman, 24; fires into 2d
 Wisconsin, 135; charges up Henry
 Hill, 140–42
North Carolina Troops
 6th: on Henry Hill, 117–19
Norris, Lt. Charles R., 27th Va.: leads
his company into battle and killed,
113, *116*

O

Ohio Troops
 2d: near the Stone Bridge, 40–41
Opie, Pvt. John, 5th Va., *90, 126, 134,
139, 143*; describes Henry Hill battle,
128; after the battle description, 174,
175
Orange and Alexandria Railroad, 17
Ott, Pvt. William, 4th Va., *111*; killed,
115

P

Parker, Pvt. Thomas, 2d R.I.: helps
carry his colonel to a field hospital, 54
Patterson, Gen. Robert: in the
Shenandoah Valley, *19*, 19, 37, 176
Payne, Capt. William H. *See* vignette,
170
Peck, Lt. Col. Harry, 2d Wis.: in battle,
135, 137
Piedmont Station, 19
Poplar Ford (Red House), 34; Map 8, 36
Porter, Col. Andrew, 54, *60*, 61, *65, 71*,
72, 177
Preston, Col. James, 4th Va., 111, 123

Q

Quinby, Col. Isaac, 13th N.Y., *132, 146*

R

Radford, Col. Richard C.W., 30th Va.
Cavalry: attacks the retreating Union
soldiers, 162, 170
Ramsay, Lt. Douglas: killed, 115, *116*
Randall, Pvt. Wesley, 27th N.Y.: killed,
78